## THE POCKET GUIDE TO
## EDINBURGH'S BEST BUILDINGS

*The Palace of Holyroodhouse and the new Scottish Parliament in the Old Town below Salisbury Crags and Arthur's Seat.*

# THE POCKET GUIDE TO
# EDINBURGH'S
# BEST BUILDINGS

### Robin Ward

First published in 2025 by Birlinn Ltd
West Newington House
10 Newington Road
Edinburgh EH9 1QS

www.birlinn.co.uk

Text, photographs and maps copyright © Robin Ward 2025
The right of Robin Ward to be identified as the author of this work has been asserted in accordance with the Copyright, Design and Patent Act 1988.

All rights reserved. No part of this publication may be reproduced, stored or transmitted in any form, or by means, electronic, mechanical or photo-copying, recording or otherwise, without the express written permission of the publisher.

ISBN 978 1 78027 923 7
*British Library Cataloguing-in-Publication Data*
A catalogue record for this book is available from the British Library

Printed and bound by PNB, Latvia

*The skyline of the Old Town with the crown steeple of St Giles' High Kirk.*

# Contents

**INTRODUCTION 7**

**BEST OF THE BEST 11**

Tour A—**HOLYROOD AND THE OLD TOWN 25**

B—**CALTON HILL, PRINCES STREET AND THE NEW TOWN 67**

C—**LOTHIAN ROAD, THE WEST END AND INVERLEITH 95**

D—**THE SOUTH SIDE 117**

E—**NEWHAVEN AND LEITH 143**

F—**BEYOND THE CITY CENTRE 161**

**INDEX 188**

# Introduction

SCOTLAND'S CAPITAL CITY is unique for its layers of historic buildings on a volcanic landscape eroded by an Ice Age glacier. There are panoramas, perspectives and sudden views – where turning corners in the medieval Old Town will reveal the spiky-roofed Gothic splendour of St Giles' High Kirk, the neoclassical New Town, the Greek Revival 'field of monuments' on Calton Hill and the North Sea. An extinct volcano, Arthur's Seat, and Edinburgh Castle loom above everything.

The Old and New Towns are separated by a glacial valley drained of its Nor' (North) Loch and landscaped in the 19th century to create Princes Street Gardens, one of the world's great urban parks. Railway tracks to Waverley Station were laid in the 1840s below Castle Rock. The station was named after the 'Waverley' novels of Sir Walter Scott. His monument, a fantastic Gothic pinnacle, punctuates the park. This terrific townscape – Castle Rock, the Old and New Towns, Calton Hill, and Princes Street Gardens – was declared in 1995 a UNESCO World Heritage Site.

This guide features the best of the city's world heritage and modern architecture along with historic sites and buildings in the

Opposite: *The Gothic Revival west front of St Giles' High Kirk is decorated with gargoyles and statues of Scottish monarchs and clerics. St Giles, Edinburgh's patron saint, appears in the shadow of the arch with the deer he is said to have saved from a hunter's arrow.*

hinterland where suburbs absorbed rural villages in the 19th and 20th centuries. The six self-guided tours are organised for walking, cycling, public transit or car, with entries numbered and keyed to maps. Monuments and sculpture are featured, especially in the city centre where, if you look up, 19th-century classical- and Renaissance-style statues stare out from façades everywhere.

Much of the Old Town is a Victorian fantasy with buildings designed in the romantic Scots Baronial style popularised by Walter Scott. The main street is the Royal Mile – Castlehill, the Lawnmarket, High Street and the Canongate – arrow-straight from the Castle to the Stuart dynasty's Palace of Holyroodhouse and the new Scottish Parliament. From 1860 to 1900, two-thirds of the medieval buildings in the Old Town were demolished for slum clearance and civic improvement, but the pattern of settlement remains. Old 'wynds' and 'closes' (the shadowy alleys and entrances to tenement courtyards) branch off perpendicular to the Royal Mile. Most were named after their builders or residents or commercial activities: for example, Advocates', Brodie's, Lady Stair's, Fishmarket, Fleshmarket, Sugarhouse. Some are said to be haunted.

Edinburgh, a clean-air city, wasn't always so. It was known as 'Auld Reekie' for the stink before modern sanitation, and for the smoke from coal fires that lingered like fog above the tenements, described by Robert Louis Stevenson as 'smoky beehives, ten stories high'. They were a response to the topography – the Old Town tumbles down a steep-sided volcanic ridge on which the only way to accommodate its citizens was to build high. By the mid 18th century, the overcrowded environment, where rich and poor scurried around amidst opulence and squalor, had become unsustainable.

Lord Provost George Drummond visualised a new town and

promoted a design competition for it. The New Town Plan of 1767 was a symbol of the Age of Enlightenment, the revival of classical culture in which Scotland played a significant role. More than any other European city, Edinburgh expressed the Enlightenment in architecture. The design of the National Monument on Calton Hill was copied from the Parthenon; the Royal Scottish Academy and the National Gallery are also classical in style. The city acquired a new nickname: 'The Athens of the North'.

Edinburgh's conventional narrative of enlightenment and cultural heritage ignores many ghosts. The most disturbing are those from the transatlantic slave trade. Sugarhouse Close was named for a refinery where sugar produced by African slaves on colonial plantations in the Caribbean was processed. Many of the plantations were owned by Scottish merchants. Profits from plantations and the wealth created by British imperialism enriched the nation. Edinburgh, like other cities and institutions, has recently acknowledged its involvement with slavery and colonial conquest.

Edinburgh World Heritage Site has so many buildings of interest listed by Historic Environment Scotland that not all could be included in this guide. Those featured have been chosen variously for their architectural qualities, social, cultural and political histories, and sustainability (meaning 'green', eco-friendly). Doors Open Days, the annual opportunity to see inside buildings not normally open to the public, are recommended. Some properties are only open in season, on weekends or for special events, notably the Edinburgh International Festival. The opening page of each tour lists personal favourites not to be missed.

*Robin Ward, Edinburgh 2025*

View from Edinburgh Castle: *Few cities reveal their social and topographical development as dramatically as Edinburgh. In all directions from Castle Rock the city is spread out like a map. Seen here (left to right) are Calton Hill with the North Sea on the horizon, the domes, spires and steeples of the Old Town, Castle Esplanade, Salisbury Crags and Arthur's Seat.*

# Best of the best

*The castle was besieged, burned and rebuilt over the centuries. The most daring exploit was its capture in 1314 by the Earl of Moray who led a band of patriots up Castle Rock at night by a secret route and seized it from the English garrison. Bonnie Prince Charlie's Jacobite army failed to capture it in 1745, the last time it was attacked.*

Edinburgh World Heritage Site seen from Calton Hill: *The contrast between the medieval Old Town and the Georgian New Town defines Edinburgh's physical character – an architectural Jekyll and Hyde. Robert Louis Stevenson stood here and noted in his narrative of the city,* Edinburgh, Picturesque Notes: *'You mount by stairs in a cutting of the*

*rock to find yourself in a field of monuments. Of all places for a view, this Calton Hill is perhaps the best.' The monument shown here, by William Playfair, architect of 'The Athens of the North', honours philosopher Dugald Stewart. The curly building on the right crowns a new layer of development, the St James Quarter.*

The Thistle Chapel: *The Order of the Thistle, Scotland's oldest and premier order of chivalry, is awarded by the monarch to Scots or people of Scots ancestry as a reward for distinguished service. The Thistle Chapel in St Giles' High Kirk is suitably decorated with religious and heraldic iconography of exceptional artistry and craftsmanship.*

Playfair Library: *This magnificent neoclassical room is a must-see in the Old College, the site where the University of Edinburgh was established in 1583. The library, a barrel-vaulted promenade lined with classical columns and busts of past professors, was named after its architect William Playfair.*

The Bank of Scotland: *Scotland's oldest bank was founded in 1695 by an Act of the Scottish Parliament. Its palatial Victorian headquarters dominates The Mound. The dome is crowned with a statue of 'Fame' above those representing Britannia and her Children, History, Geography, Navigation, Commerce, Prosperity and Plenty.*

Fettes College: *Edinburgh has several 'pauper palaces', endowed by Victorian philanthropy to educate underprivileged children. Fettes is the most extravagant of them all – a mélange of Scots Baronial and Loire château styles with a potpourri of pinnacles, statues and turrets, gargoyles, carved grape vines, serpents, birds and bees.*

McEwan Hall, the University of Edinburgh: *The most opulent graduation and concert hall in Europe and probably the only one funded by sales of beer. Its benefactor was brewery baron William McEwan. The belle-époque auditorium is as grand as any opera house. Neoclassical murals symbolising Arts and Sciences adorn the dome.*

Mansfield-Traquair Centre: *'Edinburgh's Sistine Chapel', a barrel-vaulted nave, chancel and side chapels covered with murals. The work was commissioned by the Catholic Apostolic Church whose members believed in the Second Coming of Christ. The interior was decorated accordingly by Arts and Crafts artist Phoebe Traquair.*

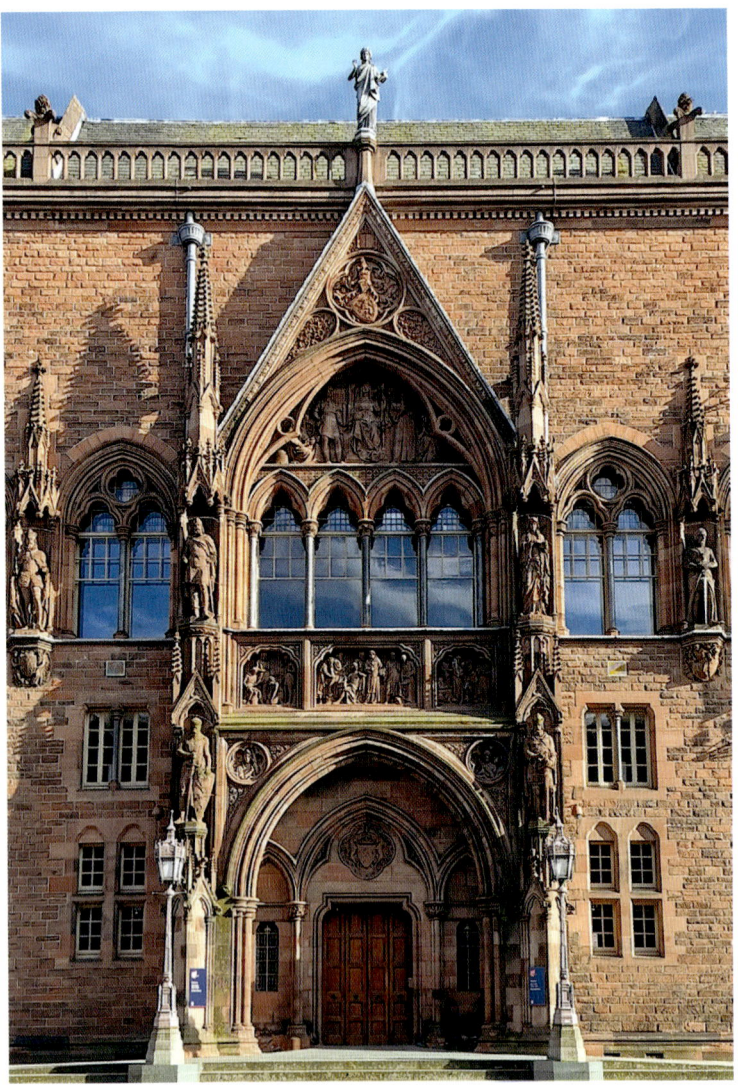

Scottish National Portrait Gallery: *Statues of William Wallace and Robert the Bruce, heroes of the Wars of Independence in the 13th and 14th centuries, guard the entrance to this Victorian palace of Scottish culture and its people. The Grand Hall, where visitors are greeted by a marble statue of Robert Burns, is decorated with dazzling murals and an astrological ceiling.*

**BEST OF THE BEST**

The new Scottish Parliament, 'democracy by design': *No other 21st-century building in Scotland has surpassed this one for complexity, cost, controversy and creativity. The office pods on the Members' Block (with visual clues to the Old Town's crow-stepped gables and oak lattice screens for shade) were conceived as 'monks' cells' to encourage the politicians to think!*

Leith Old Harbour: *Coastal and sea-going sailing ships crowded the harbour until the mid 19th century when deep-water docks were built for steamships. The once tidal haven, where the Water of Leith flowed to the sea, has been maintained at high-water level since 1968 when a barrier and lock gate were installed in the outer harbour.*

*The east quayside, known as The Shore, is picturesque with historic buildings (and new ones in heritage style). The architecture is Scottish but the scene could be Hanseatic, reflecting old Leith's trade with the nations of continental Europe, recalled in street names – Baltic, Cadiz, Elbe and Madeira.*

# Tour A
# Holyrood and the Old Town

*Holyrood Abbey*

*Palace of Holyroodhouse*

*Scottish Parliament*

*Canongate Tolbooth*

*Museum of Edinburgh*

*Scottish Storytelling Centre*

*Old St Paul's Episcopal Church*

*The Scotsman Building*

*City Art Centre*

*Fruitmarket Gallery*

*St Giles' High Kirk and the Thistle Chapel*

*Patrick Geddes Centre*

*Ramsay Garden*

*Edinburgh Castle and the National War Memorial*

*Central Library*

*Greyfriars Kirk and Kirkyard*

*George Heriot's School*

*National Museum of Scotland*

*Surgeons' Hall*

*The Old College . . .*

Opposite: *The Writers' Museum. Robert Burns, Walter Scott and Robert Louis Stevenson haunt this 17th-century house where a compelling collection of memorabilia associated with them is displayed. Their fame and the talents of other writers associated with Edinburgh led to the city being declared in 2004 the world's first UNESCO City of Literature.*

# EDINBURGH'S BEST BUILDINGS

## Tour A—HOLYROOD AND THE OLD TOWN

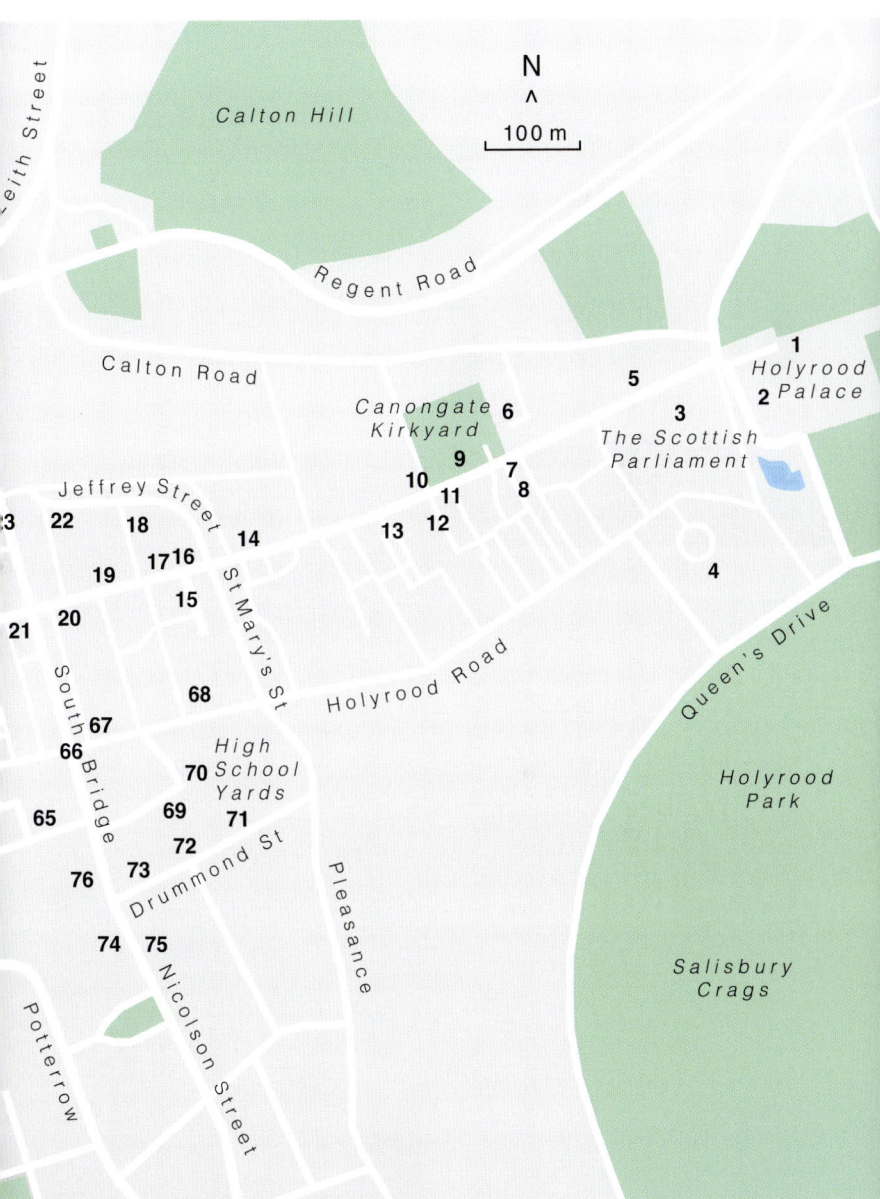

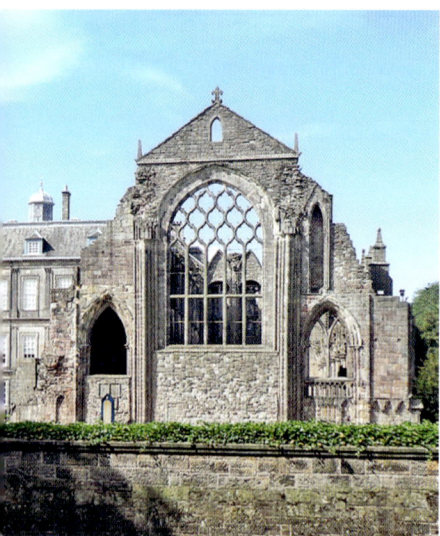

### A 1
**Holyrood Abbey**
Holyrood Park

This was the Augustinian Abbey of Holyrood (Holy Cross) founded in 1128 by King David I. Legend has it that while out hunting deer he was attacked and thrown from his horse by a stag. He seized its antlers. In a flash of sunlight they were transformed to a holy cross. That night, the king had a vision that he must build the abbey to give thanks. Over the next two centuries it was enlarged – more than twice the size seen today. Excavations in 1911 exposed foundations of long-lost transepts and a chancel.

In the 16th century, the abbey was looted and burned by the English, and the monastic regime ousted during the Protestant Reformation. The traceried east gable dates from Charles I's Scottish coronation in 1633. James VII expelled the congregation and made the nave the Chapel Royal. A mob stripped it of Catholic symbols in 1688 when James, the last Stuart monarch, was deposed.

The roof collapsed in 1768. Victorian romantics thought the ruined nave sublime. It remains as they saw it, a Gothic ghost beside the Palace of Holyroodhouse.

### A 2
**The Palace of Holyroodhouse**
Holyrood Park
*16th century; reconstructed by William Bruce 'Surveyor of the King's Buildings in Scotland' and Robert Mylne 'King's Master Mason' 1671–78*

The official residence in Scotland of the reigning British monarch who visits annually, hands out honours and hosts a garden party. But behind the ceremony and decorum there is a bloody story.

Holyroodhouse was conceived

by James IV in 1501. James V added the Northwest Tower styled like a Loire château. The palace survived when Edinburgh was invaded in the 1540s – the 'rough wooing', an attempt by Henry VIII to have his son Edward marry Mary Queen of Scots and so end the Auld Alliance between France and Scotland.

Mary is the most romantic and ill-fated royal associated with the palace. It was here, in her chambers in the Northwest Tower, that assassins led by her jealous husband Lord Darnley stabbed to death her private secretary David Rizzio. Stains on the floor are said to be his blood.

In 1603, James VI became James I of England and took the Royal Court to London. Charles II reconstructed and revived Holyroodhouse, creating the symmetrical west front. Its Doric-columned entrance with flamboyant heraldry leads to a Renaissance-style courtyard and the royal apartments. The Long Gallery features portraits of Scottish monarchs. The fountain in the forecourt is a Victorian replica of the one erected for James V at Linlithgow Palace.

### A3
**The Scottish Parliament**
Canongate
*Enric Miralles and Benedetta Tagliabue (EMBT), RMJM architects, Arup engineers 2001–2004*

Scotland's old parliament 'voted itself out of existence' in 1707

when the Act of Union with England created the British state, with its parliament in London. Repatriation of the Scottish Parliament was approved by referendum in 1997. A design competition was won by Barcelona architects EMBT. Costs and criticism spiralled as the design evolved but it was a masterpiece in the making.

The organic plan grows out of the Old Town – a 'dialogue across time' architect Miralles said. Leaf and boat shapes symbolise the land and sea of Scotland. The Debating Chamber's spectacular glulam (glue-laminated) oak trusses recall

the 17th-century timber roof of Old Parliament Hall. The Canongate Wall is a collage of poetic quotations and stones from across the nation, with a sketch by Miralles of the Old Town. A 17th-century mansion, Queensberry House, was restored as part of the project.

Sustainable features include natural ventilation, renewable energy and green roofs, even beehives (the beeswax is used for official seals). The landscape, biodiverse with native plants and flowers, blends with historic Holyrood Park.

A 4
**Dynamic Earth**
Holyrood Road
*Michael Hopkins & Partners 1999*

A fabric-skinned pavilion like some prehistoric creature lodged in the shell of a 19th-century brewery. The brewery walls, visible on Queen's Drive, were disguised as a castle to please Queen Victoria.

The style is High Tech with the roof cable-stayed from steel pylons. Exhibits inside feature Planet Earth. James Hutton, 'the founder of modern geology', lived

nearby. Directly south are volcanic features that inspired him, Salisbury Crags and Arthur's Seat.

A 5
**White Horse Close**
27 Canongate

Looks like a film set but the buildings are real enough, restored in the 1960s. The close was known for the White Horse Inn where stagecoaches departed to and arrived from London.

During the Jacobite rising of 1745, Bonnie Prince Charlie's officers lodged here while the prince occupied Holyroodhouse. The name of the close refers to a white horse said to have been stabled here for Mary Queen of Scots.

A 6
**Adam Smith's Panmure House**
4 Lochend Close, Canongate

Built in 1691 when the Canongate was a rural, aristocratic suburb of the Old Town. The owner was the Earl of Panmure, a Jacobite who forfeited the property to the British state after the failed rising of 1715.

In 1778, Adam Smith, author of

*The Wealth of Nations*, moved in. Among those drawn to his 'salons' were architect Robert Adam, chemist Joseph Black, geologist James Hutton and philosopher Dugald Stewart.

Their spirit of enquiry inspired the restoration of the house for Heriot-Watt University in 2018 as a forum for economic and social debate. Smith's elaborate tomb can be found in Canongate Kirkyard.

### A 7
**112 Canongate**
*Richard Murphy Architects 1999*

This Saltire Society Housing Design Award winner in 2000 was built for the Old Town Housing Association. Timber siding and harled walls evoke the past, along with upper rooms cantilevered from the façade to gain floor space, a typical feature of medieval housing in Edinburgh. The typographic message, 'A nation is forged in the hearth of poetry', recalls instructive texts seen on buildings in the Old Town.

In nearby Dunbar's Close is a 17th-century style garden such

as would have been enjoyed by Canongate's aristocratic residents.

### A 8
**Scottish Poetry Library**
5 Crichton's Close, Canongate
*Malcolm Fraser Architects 1999*

Award-winning architecture in an alley of mixed-up buildings (tenements and an old brewery). Outdoor steps were used as seats for readings – poetry *en plein air*. Unfortunately, this liberating feature was lost when the library, needing more space on the tight site, was enlarged in 2015.

### A 9
**Canongate Kirk**
153 Canongate

'Canongate' refers not to a gate, but *gait* from the Norse word for 'street' where walked the canons of Holyrood Abbey. James VII built the kirk in 1688 for the congregation he evicted from the abbey which he wanted for the Chapel Royal. Funds were from merchant Thomas Moodie, noted on architect James Smith's Dutch-gabled façade.

Above the rose window is the coat of arms of William of Orange, who took the British throne from James VII. The antlers on top of the gable symbolise the stag in the founding story of Holyrood Abbey. The interior is festooned with royal and regimental banners and flags, this being the Kirk of Holyroodhouse and Edinburgh Castle.

The statue of poet Robert Fergusson striding past the kirk was placed here in 2004. Fergusson was buried in the kirkyard in an unmarked grave. Robert Burns found it 'unnoticed and unknown' in 1787 and paid for a headstone inscribed with an elegy he wrote.

### A 10
**Canongate Tolbooth**
163 Canongate

Built in 1591, this was the town hall, jail and courthouse of the old Burgh of Canongate which was absorbed by Edinburgh in 1856. The style is Franco-Scottish – the architecture of the Auld Alliance. The 'forestair' from the street led to the council chamber and courtroom; the jail was in the tower.

On the façade is the burgh's coat of arms dated 1128 (when Holyrood Abbey was founded). Inscriptions in Latin read: 'Justice, piety, truth, thus is the way to the stars'

and 'For Native Land and Posterity 1591'. The Victorian attic windows have star and thistle finials. The clock on wrought-iron brackets was installed in 1884; the tavern dates from 1820. The Tolbooth houses Edinburgh Museums' The People's Story.

A 11
**The Museum of Edinburgh**
140–146 Canongate

'The city's treasure box' is housed in several buildings, principally the gabled medieval Huntly House named after the Marquess of Huntly.

Originally timber, the house was reconstructed with masonry in 1570. Latin inscriptions on the façade lent the property a nickname: 'The Talking House'. Bought by the City of Edinburgh in 1924, it is now a museum, a labyrinth to get pleasurably lost in.

Huntly House, Canongate Kirk and the Tolbooth form the largest cluster of 16th- and 17th-century urban buildings in Scotland. Among them is Acheson House in Bakehouse Close. The original owner was Archibald Acheson, a government minister. In the 19th century the close was a slum and Acheson House a tenement and brothel. Today, it is occupied by Edinburgh World Heritage.

A 12
**Sugarhouse Close**
154–166 Canongate

The name sounds sweet but hides the bitter taste of Scotland's role in the slave trade. The Edinburgh Sugar House Company opened a refinery here in 1752. The raw material came from plantations worked by African slaves in the Caribbean.

From 1829 to 1852, the refinery was owned by William Macfie & Co., a sugar dynasty established in 1788 at Greenock (Port Glasgow). Above the entrance is a panel with the Clan Macfie lion rampant and

motto *Pro Rege* meaning 'For the King'. The close was redeveloped as a brewery in the 1860s and recently as student housing.

A 13
**Moray House**
174 Canongate

Now the main academic office of the University of Edinburgh's Moray House School of Education, this is the finest of old Canongate's aristocratic townhouses. It was built c. 1620 for the Countess of Home whose coat of arms is above the corbelled balcony on Canongate. Her daughter, the Countess of Moray, inherited the property in 1645.

The garden once extended to what is now Holyrood Road, from where you can see the Summer House. Inside, according to Walter Scott, the 'false and corrupted statesmen' who signed the 1707 Act of Union with England 'were obliged to hold their meetings in secret, lest they should have been assaulted by the rabble [of protesters].' Most Scots opposed the treaty but they had no vote. Robert Burns, in a poem of 1791, wrote that the aristocrats who signed it had been bribed and the nation 'sold for English gold'.

A 14
**Morocco Land**
265 Canongate

This 17th-century tenement was rebuilt in the 1950s after part of it collapsed. Reconstruction salvaged its unique feature – the statue on the façade of a Moor.

Urban myth says it represents Andrew Gray, a fugitive from justice after assaulting the Lord Provost of Edinburgh. He escaped to the Barbary Coast where he found favour and fortune with the Sultan of Morocco.

Eventually, he returned with a crew of pirates and threatened to loot the city. He was pardoned after volunteering to cure the Lord Provost's daughter of the plague, married her and settled here.

Good story, but the Moor on the

façade was more likely to have advertised a Morocco leather dealer or a bookbinder.

## A 15
**Tweeddale Court**
14 High Street

A wrought-iron gate at the end of the close opens to a courtyard and Tweeddale House (c. 1576), named for the Marquess of Tweeddale who bought it in 1670. The British Linen Bank acquired the property in 1791. The courtyard was a crime scene in 1806 when a bank messenger was murdered and robbed of £4,000. Most of the cash was found hidden in a wall not far away but the killer was not caught. Later owners of the house included printers Oliver & Boyd whose name is above the door.

Also in the courtyard is a fragment of the King's Wall, a fortification built by James II that once marked the limits of the Old Town. Attached to it is an 18th-century shed used for storing sedan chairs on which the well-to-do could be carried so as not to set foot on the town's filthy streets.

## A 16
**Scottish Storytelling Centre**
43–45 High Street
*Malcolm Fraser Architects 2006*

An award-winning retrofit of the 1970s Netherbow Arts Centre, inspired by an old Scottish proverb: 'The story is told eye to eye, mind to mind and heart to heart.'

The intervention, with a forestair and 'outlook' tower, incorporates the historic John Knox House. The centre's tower recalls Netherbow Port, the most impressive of the Old Town's six medieval gates. The panel with the legend '1606, God save the King' on the wall of the tower is a relic of the gate's reconstruction (a carving on the façade of the adjacent tenement shows how it looked).

The gate was demolished in 1764 because it was no longer needed for defence and was too narrow for the increase in traffic. Its clock was later attached to Dean Orphanage (now the National Gallery Modern Two building). Its bell, cast in the Netherlands in 1621, hangs in a niche at the top of the Storytelling Centre's tower.

### A 17
**John Knox House and Moubray House**
43–45 and 51–53 High Street

Dating back to 1470, the John Knox House is the oldest medieval building on the Royal Mile. Knox, the preacher of the Scottish Reformation, is said to have lived here, a link which saved the house from demolition in the 19th century.

The property was once the home of Mariota Arres whose husband, James Mossman, was goldsmith to Mary Queen of Scots. The couple's initials are visible outside along with a sundial, a figure (Moses, not John Knox) receiving God's wisdom, and an inscription, 'Luve God abuve al and yi nychtbour as yi self'. Mossman's loyalty to Mary Queen of Scots led to his execution in 1573.

Set back next door is Moubray House (1477; reconstructed in 1529). It was restored in 1910 by the Cockburn Association. The association, founded in 1875, is named after lawyer and conservationist Lord Henry Cockburn who had campaigned to save the John Knox House.

### A 18
**Trinity Apse**
Chalmers Close

Trinity College Kirk was removed stone-by-stone in 1848 to make way for Waverley Station. The stones were numbered and stored for re-erection. While plans to rebuild the kirk on Calton Hill, Castle Rock or in Princes Street Gardens came and went, builders stole much of the masonry, leaving 'a medieval jigsaw puzzle'.

In 1877, the remaining stones were used to rebuild the apse, attached to a new church. When that church was demolished in 1964 the apse was spared. It is a marvel of medieval masons' craft,

lofty and fan-vaulted. Numbered stones can still be spotted. The south wall faces a garden where stones carved as gargoyles, a monster's feet and the Green Man are scattered.

### A 19
**Heave Awa' House**
Paisley Close, 101 High Street

One night in 1861, a 250-year old tenement here collapsed killing 35 of the 77 residents. In the rubble the next morning a boy's voice was heard by rescuers: 'Heave awa' lads, ah'm no' deid yet'.

When the close was rebuilt in 1862, his release was honoured. His face, serene considering how he got here, is on the keystone. The tragedy and the hazardous state of other tenements led to the City Improvement Act of 1867, slum clearances and reconstruction, typically in Scots Baronial style.

### A 20
**Radisson Blu Hotel**
80 High Street

A Scots Baronial parody with pitched roofs, gables, and turreted

drum towers that look like they walked up the Royal Mile from the Palace of Holyroodhouse.

Built in 1990 as the Scandic Crown Hotel, its architect Ian Begg recalled that the Danish client 'wanted a building of strong character to make clear that it was in Scotland, people visiting had to be in no doubt where they were'. Lest anyone be deceived by its antique appearance, the date is on a plaque at the Niddry Street corner.

### A 21
**The Tron Kirk**
122 High Street
*John Mylne master mason; John Scott master wright 1637–47*

Presbyterians displaced when Charles I made St Giles' High Kirk a cathedral received this compensation from the king.

During the Great Fire of 1824 it was showered with flying embers which burned the Dutch style, lead-clad timber bell tower. The façades and the timber hammer beam roof were spared. The

tower was rebuilt in stone above the original Roman Doric vestibule which can still be seen. The stained glass windows are Victorian.

Part of the kirk was demolished in the 1780s when South Bridge was constructed. After worship ceased in 1952 the building was acquired by the City. Archaeological excavations revealed traces inside of Marlin's Wynd, the earliest paved street in Scotland. The kirk's name comes from the 'tron', a public weigh beam for salt and other commodities once nearby.

A 22
**Old St Paul's Episcopal Church**
39 Jeffrey Street

The plain Gothic exterior of 1883 suggests nothing worth seeing here, but Old St Paul's has one of the city's finest ecclesiastical interiors. A door in Carrubber's Close opens directly into the nave, or you can enter from the street and climb the Calvary Stair. The stair, constructed in 1926 along with the War Memorial Chapel, has 33 steps to mark each year of Christ's life.

Inside, there are painted panels like Florentine frescoes and a trio of stained glass windows depicting Saint Paul, The Crucifixion and Saint Columba. The War Memorial Chapel displays the Martyrs' Cross, a small iron cross originally attached to a house opposite the gallows on the Grassmarket. It was the last thing seen by the condemned, among them Scottish Episcopalians persecuted for supporting the Jacobites.

A 23
**The Scotsman Building**
North Bridge
*Dunn & Findlay architects*
*Redpath, Brown & Co. engineers*
*1900–1904*

This was the beating heart of *The Scotsman* newspaper's empire, identified by 'The Scotsman'

emblem on the north façade. The logo's thistle was chosen not only because it is Scotland's national plant but also because it is spiky and sharp, as the paper's founders set out to be in 1817.

Sculptures of Mercury the messenger and Night and Day (after Michelangelo) animate the stonework on the 11-storey, steel-framed vertically organised complex. An opulent lobby, editorial offices and the newsroom were at North Bridge; below were composing (typesetting) and the press room where the paper was printed; dispatch was on Market Street.

The 'pagoda of publishing excellence' was part of a project that included flats above shops and North Bridge Arcade, a once elegant Parisian style covered shopping passage between North Bridge and Cockburn Street. The arcade is one of the few of its type to survive in Scotland.

In 1998, the owners of *The Scotsman* sold their building. It is now The Scotsman Hotel. The paper's name on the façade had to be kept as part of the building's Category A-listed heritage.

A 24
### The Scotsman Steps
*Dunn & Findlay 1899*

The steps provide a pedestrian link between North Bridge and Market Street in an octagonal tower derived from the spiral staircase at the Château Royal de Blois in France. The tower was restored by the City and Edinburgh World Heritage in 2011. The 104 steps, eroded by footsteps over a century, were resurfaced, each with marble sourced from around the world by artist Martin Creed, commissioned by the Fruitmarket Gallery.

### A 25
**Fruitmarket Gallery**
45 Market Street

Founded in 1974, this contemporary art gallery is named for its building, a 1930s former fruit and vegetable warehouse. The structure is supported on a massive steel truss girder visible from inside Waverley Station where produce was transferred from trains.

The gallery was refreshed by Richard Murphy Architects (1993) with a butterfly roof and minimalist, skylit exhibition space upstairs. In 2021, more space was opened next door, also a former produce warehouse. Architects Reiach & Hall revealed and retained its Victorian industrial aesthetic.

### A 26
**City Art Centre**
2 Market Street

This was originally a warehouse built as part of *The Scotsman* newspaper complex. The six floors were retrofitted in 1980 for the City's diverse collection of Scottish art dating from 17th century and for temporary exhibitions. The

makeover created a luminous and welcoming double-height foyer.

### A 27
**Waverley Cafe**
Market Street at Waverley Bridge
*Ebenezer James McRae 1933*

One of many police telephone boxes made at the Carron Foundry, Falkirk for the City of Edinburgh – tiny temples, inspired by the city's

Greek Revival architecture. Originally they were painted police blue. Decommissioned, some have been reused like this one which is heritage-listed.

## A 28
**The Tattoo Office**
1–3 Cockburn Street

'An experience like no other', the Royal Edinburgh Military Tattoo has been performed on Edinburgh Castle's Esplanade since 1950. Its office suites occupy the former Cockburn Hotel, named for Henry Cockburn whose portrait in stone can be seen above the door. The ghost sign on the lintel recalls the hotel's proprietor, John Macpherson. The building is one of several here erected in the 1860s in the fashionable Scots Baronial style.

## A 29
**Fleshmarket Close**

Bisected by Cockburn Street, the close connects the Royal Mile to Market Street. It was named for the Flesh Market – the slaughterhouse and meat market beside the Nor'

Loch at the foot of the close long before Waverley Station was built.

## A 30
**Old Fishmarket Close**
190 High Street

Henry Cockburn called this 'a steep, narrow stinking ravine' where fish had been sold since the 16th century, not in the most sanitary conditions. Town council's cleansing of the Royal Mile forced the fishmongers and other traders to public markets below North Bridge, where Waverley Station is today. The only fish here now are

on an artwork where seven swim across the archway.

The close plunges down to the Cowgate passing two buildings by Richard Murphy Architects, with old-style timber gables and harled walls fitting the historic context.

## A 31
**City Chambers**
253 High Street
*John and Robert Adam 1753–61*

In 1811, the town council moved out of the medieval Old Tolbooth beside St Giles' High Kirk and into the Royal Exchange, which had been the first of Lord Provost George Drummond's improvement projects. Inside, it had a customs office, coffee house and spaces for merchants to trade. After the town council took it over it was rebranded the City Chambers.

The sculpture in the courtyard, *Alexander and Bucephalus* by Sir John Steell, was relocated

here in 1916 from St Andrew Square where it had been since 1884. It shows the horse Bucephalus spooked by its shadow and Alexander the Great turning it towards the sun to tame it.

## A 32
**St Giles' High Kirk**
High Street

The 12th-century Romanesque kirk was looted and burned during the invasion of Scotland in 1385 by English king Richard II. Rebuilt and enlarged over the following centuries it stands like island of stone pinnacles. The open space here dates from the early 19th century when the Old Tolbooth and traders' stalls called 'Luckenbooths' (thought to mean locked at night) were demolished.

Around 1830, William Burn gave the kirk a Gothic Revival facelift. Looking at the alterations some decades later, Robert Louis Stevenson condemned 'zealous magistrates and a misguided architect' and that the church 'if it were not for the spire, would be unrecognisable'. The spire is one of three 'crown steeples' from the Middle Ages to survive in Scotland (the others are in Aberdeen and Glasgow).

The kirk was stripped of its Catholic symbols during the Reformation. Charles I in 1633, the year of his Scottish coronation, proclaimed it a cathedral. Lord Provost William Chambers, in 1871, commissioned a restoration

of the pre-Reformation volume. A Gothic Revival west front by architect William Hay and sculptor John Rhind was completed in 1884 (photo, page 6). The larger-than-life statue of the 5th Duke of Buccleuch outside was unveiled in 1888.

The interior is theatrical with a cast of characters, among them effigies of John Knox, the kirk's minister during the Reformation, the Marquess of Montrose and Marquess of Argyll, enemies during the civil wars of the 17th century, and even Robert Louis Stevenson. Trade guilds are represented by their respective saints on the screen to the north transept. Contrasting with the kirk's traditional decoration is the Robert Burns Memorial Window (1985) above the west door.

A 33
**The Thistle Chapel, St Giles' High Kirk**
*Robert Lorimer 1910*

Scotland's pre-eminent order of chivalry, the Order of the Thistle, was revived in 1687 by James VII who created a chapel at Holyrood Abbey for its knights. They lost it when the king was deposed in

1688. The order was dormant until 1703 and without a chapel until this one was built snug against the great kirk of St Giles'. The preferred site was the abbey ruin but it would not support a new roof.

The style is 15th-century Gothic, with an Arts and Crafts decorative scheme crowned with a fan-vaulted ceiling packed with ornament, like jewels in a box. Shining among them are carved ceiling bosses, heraldic emblems and angels, some playing bagpipes.

A 34
**Mercat Cross**
Parliament Square

The Mercat (market) Cross of 1617 was where royal and civic proclamations were made and where merchants preferred to meet, even after the Royal Exchange was provided for them. It was declared an obstruction to traffic in 1756 and 'utterly destroyed by a misguided hand'.

So wrote William Ewart Gladstone who paid for this replica. The unicorn, a traditional symbol of Scottish royalty, was carved in 1869; the column on which it sits is a reproduction from 1970. On top are carved dragons and foliage believed to have been recycled in 1617 from an earlier cross.

In 1750, a visitor stood here and said (of the Scottish Enlightenment) that he could 'in a few minutes, take 50 men of genius and learning by the hand.' Among the men of genius were David Hume and Adam Smith. A statue of Smith is here; Hume too, nearby.

A 35
**Charles II Monument**
Parliament Square

Between Old Parliament House and St Giles' High Kirk, neither

symbols of royal authority, King Charles II rides forth like a Roman emperor, seemingly disdainful of the setting. The statue (1685), cast in lead, is attributed to Dutch sculptor Grinling Gibbons. It is the city's oldest. On the stone plinth is a tribute in Latin which translated declares: 'To Charles the Second, most august and most magnificent, the invincible ruler of Britain, France and Ireland, upon whose birth Divine Providence smiled.'

A 36
### Old Parliament Hall
Old Parliament House, Parliament Square
*James Murray 'Principal Master of all His Majesties works in Scotland', John Scott master wright 1632–40*

Behind a neoclassical façade is this magnificent hall, the first purpose-built debating chamber for the Scottish Parliament and the oldest of its type in the British Isles. With an oak trussed roof, it is virtually all that is left of the original Jacobean-style building.

Old Parliament House was the town's finest civic edifice. It was commissioned by Charles I to house the Parliament, Privy Council and Court of Session. Its Renaissance-style doorway was adorned with the royal insignia and statues of Mercy and Justice. The statues, removed around 1805 when most of the building was torn down, were thought lost until spotted in an antiquarian's garden

in the New Town and returned.

After the Act of Union of 1707 the hall was used by the courts and for public functions. The stained glass South Window (1868) shows James V in 1532 establishing the Court of Session (the supreme civil court), the foundation of Scotland's legal system.

A 37
### Signet Library
Parliament Square
*William Stark 1812–22*

This was the Advocates Library, part of the old Scottish Parliament complex that houses the Supreme Courts of Scotland. When the advocates moved to a new library in the 1830s the old one was taken over by the Society of Writers to the Signet (writers of documents sealed with the Signet, the personal seal of Scottish monarchs).

There are two neoclassical-style

rooms. The lower one is now a palatial tearoom. The upper room, a vaulted promenade lined with Corinthian columns, has a dome with painted figures of Apollo and the Muses, poets, philosophers and historians. A stained glass window commemorates the Golden Jubilee of Queen Victoria.

## A 38
### David Hume statue
High Street

'Philosopher and Historian, Scot and European. Man of the Enlightenment' are inscribed on the plinth where sits the hero of the Scottish

Enlightenment dressed like an ancient philosopher. Passersby rub his big toe, perhaps for wisdom or good luck.

The tribute was commissioned from sculptor Alexander Stoddart by the Saltire Society to mark its 60th anniversary.

## A 39
### Institut Français Écosse
West Parliament Square and George IV Bridge

This 'little corner of France in the heart of Edinburgh' was Midlothian County Buildings, later Lothian Chambers. The façade on West Parliament Square has tableaux illustrating the county's economy – agriculture, fishing and (at the time) coal mining.

The interior, evocative of Edwardian civic pride, was refurbished in 2017 for the French Consulate and the French Institute in Scotland. Their presence in Edinburgh's old royal, religious and parliamentary quarter recalls the Auld Alliance, the royal, military and cultural bond that lasted from the Franco-Scottish treaty of 1295 until the Reformation. The institute hosts visual arts and music, and has a library, language school, diplomatic offices and, naturally, a bistro.

## A 40
### Bank of Scotland Headquarters
North Bank Street
*Richard Crichton and Robert Reid 1802–06; David Bryce 1864–70*

The Bank of Scotland strides into the Old Town, mounted on a massive podium on which stood the head office built in 1806. Below the dome is the bank's coat of arms with figures of Abundance and Justice, retained when architect David Bryce replaced all but the podium of the original building.

Bryce's Victorian reconstruction gave the bank tremendous visual presence. The north side (photo, page 16) is a pageant of pediments, cupolas, classical columns and symbolic statuary. The governor and directors could gaze at the view of the New Town and feel they ruled the world. The bank's history is told in the Museum on the Mound (entrance downhill on North Bank Street).

## A 41
### Deacon Brodie's Tavern
435 Lawnmarket

The tavern, opened in 1806 in an 18th-century tenement, is named after Deacon Brodie, 'respected citizen by day, burglar at night'. His double life is said to have inspired Robert Louis Stevenson's novel *The Strange Case of Dr Jekyll and Mr Hyde.*

Brodie was eventually charged with breaking into the General Excise Office at Chessel's Court on the Canongate. He escaped to the Netherlands where he was caught, returned to Edinburgh, tried and hanged in 1788. Across the Lawnmarket is Brodie's Close, named for the infamous deacon's ancestors who lived there.

A 42
**Lady Stair's House**
Lady Stair's Close

The house was built in 1622 for merchant William Gray and his wife Geida Smith. Their initials are carved on the door lintel; also the date and a sermon in stone: 'Fear the Lord and depart from Evil'. The name refers to an 18th-century resident, Elizabeth, Dowager Countess of Stair.

The Scots Baronial tower dates from a makeover in 1897 for the 5th Earl of Rosebery. He gave the building to the City in 1907 as a history museum, subsequently The Writers' Museum (see page 25). It overlooks Makars' (Poets') Court where paving stones are inscribed with quotes from Scottish writers. Robert Burns stayed nearby on his first visit to the city in 1786.

A 43
**Gladstone's Land**
477b Lawnmarket

The archaic 'land' in Scots means a tenement or apartment house. This example (c. 1550) was bought by merchant Thomas Gledstanes in 1617 for improvement to attract wealthy tenants. He added an arcade for shops at street level and extended the upper floors behind a new façade. He lived on the main floor and rented out flats upstairs, a social strata typical of the Old Town.

In 1934, the once-fashionable tenement was declared 'unfit for human habitation'. It was saved from demolition, becoming the first property bought by National Trust for Scotland. Restoration uncovered decorated painted ceilings in three rooms created when

Thomas Gledstanes reconstructed the building. His surname inspired the NTS sign outside – the bird of prey catching a rat is a modelled on a 'glede' (kite or hawk), an image of which appears on the ceiling in Gledstanes' former flat.

### A 44
**Patrick Geddes Centre**
Riddle's Close and Court
322 Lawnmarket

Step through the close off the Lawnmarket and you are suddenly intimate with late 16th-century Edinburgh, when Riddle's Court was owned by Bailie MacMorran, a merchant with royal connections. A plaque notes: 'In the court beyond Bailie MacMorran banqueted in his house James VI, his queen [Anna of Denmark] and Danish nobles.'

The close runs through an 18th-century tenement built by George Riddle, a wright and burgess. His name and an eroded date (1888–95) on the archway are from renovation of Riddle's Court by conservationist and sociologist Patrick Geddes, as halls of residence for the University of Edinburgh.

Geddes advocated an organic patchwork of urban renewal keeping existing fabric where practical. His spirit informed recent work by the Scottish Historic Buildings Trust, to create a learning and cultural centre (LDN Architects 2015–17). Geddes' crest and motto, *Vivendo Discimus* meaning 'by living we learn', can be seen above the doorway in the courtyard.

### A 45
**The Ensign Ewart**
521–523 Lawnmarket

A tavern since 1680 and one of the few to retain a name from the Napoleonic Wars, a custom once common. Ensign Ewart of the Royal Scots Dragoon Guards (Scots Greys) famously seized the bronze eagle emblem of Napoleon's 45th Infantry Regiment at the Battle of Waterloo. A granite memorial to him is on Castle Esplanade. The 'Waterloo Eagle' is displayed in Royal Scots Dragoons Museum at the castle.

Tolbooth St John's eventually became an events 'hub', opened in 1999 with offices for the Edinburgh International Festival. Inside is the Sculpture Stair with more than 200 plaster figures on shelves representing past performances at the festival.

A 47
**Outlook Tower**
Castlehill

In 1853, Maria Short, daughter of Thomas Short, remodelled this 17th-century tenement. Her father had opened the first observatory on Calton Hill. Maria built her own one there. The town council thought it an eyesore and evicted her, so she relocated Maria Short's Observatory here and made it look like a castle.

Patrick Geddes bought it in 1892 and renamed it Outlook Tower. Housed in the belvedere is

A 46
**The Hub**
Castlehill
*James Gillespie Graham and Augustus Welby Pugin 1839–44*

The steeple by Pugin was intended for his St George's Cathedral, Southwark in London but not built there, to Edinburgh's benefit. At 73 metres high, the steeple is a landmark visible from miles away.

The building, originally Victoria Hall, was a place of prayer and where the General Assembly of the Church of Scotland met. When its members moved across Castlehill in 1929 to the former Free Church Hall, Victoria Hall became Highland Tolbooth St John's Church where worshipped Gaelic and English-speaking congregations. In 1979, they joined Greyfriars Kirk.

a camera obscura, which was the main attraction at Maria Short's Observatory. The tower is now the Camera Obscura and World of Illusions.

A 48
**Ramsay Garden**
Ramsay Lane

A bonny block of flats from the 1890s in Arts and Crafts style built by Patrick Geddes. He had bought Ramsey Lodge, the 'Goose Pie' house of poet Allan Ramsay, as part of the project which provided housing for staff and students at the University of Edinburgh. Geddes himself and his family lived here in a flat facing Castle Esplanade at the top of the Royal Mile.

Artist John Duncan decorated some of Ramsay Garden's interiors (now privately owned apartments) with murals of Celtic myths. He designed Witches Well, a drinking fountain set in the wall by the Esplanade. It recalls people accused of witchcraft, most of them women, who were burned at the stake here in the 16th and 17th centuries.

A 49
**Cannonball House**
Castlehill

Stuck in the stonework facing the Esplanade is a cannon ball fired by the castle's gunners at Bonnie Prince Charlie's army in 1745.

So the story goes; or the ball marks the elevation of Comiston Springs, the source of the city's first reliable water supply, following a Scottish Parliament Act in 1621 'to bring the sweet waters of the country to the centre of Edinburgh'. Pipes were laid by a Dutch engineer hired by the town council to supply public wellheads. The water was stored underground in Castlehill Reservoir (now the Tartan Weaving Mill).

A 50
**Edinburgh Castle**

Bronze statues of heroes William Wallace and Robert the Bruce guard the castle gateway (Wallace on the north side of the arch and Bruce to the south). Above the arch is the Royal Standard and a banner with the Latin motto of Scottish

monarchs: *Nemo Me Impune Lacessit,* 'No one attacks me with impunity'.

The castle is approached from an 18th-century parade ground, the Esplanade, lined with monuments from an era when kilted Highlanders were shock troops of the British Empire. A steep climb leads to Queen Margaret's Chapel (12th century, the oldest building in Edinburgh), the Royal Palace and Great Hall (both 16th century), the National War Museum and the National War Memorial; also the One o'Clock Gun and Mons Meg, a giant 15th-century siege gun. The most formidable fortification is the 16th-century Half Moon Battery, so-called for its shape.

The Great Hall, built by James IV for ceremonies and banquets, retains its original timber hammer beam roof. The palace contains the Honours of Scotland – the crown, sceptre and sword of state. The crown was made for James V and later worn by Mary Queen of Scots at her coronation in 1543.

The castle's narrow gateway, built to keep enemies out, now admits around two million visitors annually.

A 51
**Scottish National War Memorial**
Edinburgh Castle
*1923–27*

Architect Robert Lorimer, chosen by competition, visualised this memorial to the 'fallen' of the First

World War as a 'sturdy, massive type of Scotch Gothic with external buttresses rising out of the rock'. *The Scotsman* published an image showing how the castle's skyline would be 'vandalised'. The committee overseeing the project retreated and Lorimer reworked the design.

An 18th-century barracks block was gutted and given a new façade in Scottish Renaissance style, inspired by the royal palace at Stirling Castle. The Lion and Unicorn guard the entrance, above which a phoenix rises from the flames, and a sculpture symbolises 'The Survival of the Spirit'.

Lorimer deployed 200 artists and artisans to create sculptures, friezes and stained glass honouring Scottish soldiers, sailors, nurses and airmen – even the animals and carrier pigeons used by the forces.

In the Shrine, a casket contains the Rolls of Honour which list by name the dead: more than 148,000. Suspended above it is a carving in oak of God's soldier the Archangel Michael symbolising, as was hoped at the time, 'mankind's triumph over the evil of war'. Most evocative of time and memory is the summit of Castle Rock itself, exposed on the Shrine's floor.

A 52
**The Grassmarket**
Between West Port and Cowgate

'Cowgate' was the name of a cattle drovers' trail to the market established in 1477 by royal charter. Horses and cattle were traded at fairs (the 'grass' in the name refers to fodder in their pens).

This being the Old Town, there are ghosts aplenty: murderers Burke and Hare drinking at the White Hart Inn; John Porteous, Captain of the Town Guard, dragged from Old Tolbooth jail

and lynched by a mob after his men had shot dead nine citizens in a crowd attending the hanging of a smuggler; and 100 Covenanters executed during the 'killing times' of the 17th century – a circle of granite setts marks the spot, at the east end of the Grassmarket. At the west end is West Port, named for one of the gates to the Old Town in the 16th-century Flodden Wall.

### A 53
**Dance Base**
14-16 Grassmarket
*Malcolm Fraser Architects 2001*

The dance centre and its studios are choreographed on a precipitous site below the castle. The entrance, next door to the Black Bull tavern, lures you up through the layered complex, each transition defined by activity and architectural ability. A rubble-stone relic of the Flodden Wall lines the corridor that connects the reception area to roof decks and Studio 3, a perfectly proportioned Zen-like space.

Dance Base won the inaugural RIAS Andrew Doolan Award, Best Building in Scotland 2002 and was a Stirling Prize finalist that year.

### A 54
**Victoria Street**

The steeply sloping street and its elevated promenade (Victoria Terrace) were planned and built following the City Improvement Act of 1827, passed by council to sweep away slums (a second such Act was required in 1867).

Most of historic West Bow, a zigzag wynd between the Royal Mile and the Grassmarket, was amputated. Where what's left of West Bow meets the Grassmarket, you can see a 17th-century wellhead which provided citizens with fresh water (four more can be spotted on the Royal Mile).

### A 55
**Central Library**
George IV Bridge

Above the entrance of this people's palace styled like a French Renais-

sance château by architect George Washington Browne are the words 'Let there be Light' – the motto of Scottish American steel baron Andrew Carnegie who laid the foundation stone in 1887. He said free public libraries were a 'cradle of democracy' and funded more than 2,500 worldwide (the first in 1883, in his home town, Dunfermline).

He is honoured here, depicted in a sculpture in a niche on the staircase that leads to the domed Reference Library on the top floor.

A 56
**National Library of Scotland**
George IV Bridge
*Reginald Fairlie 1934–56*

This steel-framed, stone-clad library is much larger than it looks. Below street level there are seven floors of storage for millions of books, manuscripts and other printed material. It is the nation's largest reference library, established in 1925 to house the Advocates Library collection.

Completion of the building was delayed by the Second World War. Art Deco statues on the façade symbolise Medicine, Science, History, Literature, Law, Theology and Music.

A 57
**Augustine United Church**
41 George IV Bridge
*1857–61*

An exotic addition to the city's skyline with a triple-tiered tower that was likened to a wedding cake, or inspired by the Giralda tower of Seville Cathedral.

The architects, William Hardie Hay and James Murdoch Hay, were challenged by the narrow site that plunges below George IV Bridge. They failed to fit buttresses to support the walls. Architect David Bryce was called in to reinforce the structure to prevent its collapse. The church was built for members of the Congregational Church whose previous chapel was demolished to make way for the Royal Scottish Museum.

A 58
**Greyfriars Kirk**
Candlemaker Row

The original kirk, a plain building with a stumpy tower, opened in 1620 as the first new church in the town since the Reformation. The name comes from a Franciscan (Greyfriars) friary established here in 1477. The friary was looted and destroyed by Protestant reformers in 1559. Its land became a burial ground where Greyfriars Kirk was later built.

The kirk was a barracks in 1650s for Oliver Cromwell's invading army. Gunpowder stored by the Town Guard exploded in 1718 destroying the tower. The 'double' entrance porch was built in 1721 with doors for two separate congregations. A fire in 1845 gutted the interior. Reconstruction featured stained glass windows (the first in a Presbyterian church in Edinburgh since the Reformation) and a pipe organ – controversial, because music and decoration were

associated with Catholic worship.

The kirk's memorabilia includes an original copy of the National Covenant, signed here in 1638 to oppose Charles II's 'divine right' to impose Catholicism across Scotland.

A 59
**Greyfriars Bobby**
Candlemaker Row
*William Brodie sculptor 1873*

Edinburgh's most popular sculpture – the bronze effigy of the legendary Skye terrier who kept a 14-year vigil by his master's grave

in Greyfriars Kirkyard.

When the town council decreed stray dogs be caught and killed, William Chambers bought Bobby a protective collar, inscribed: 'Greyfriars Bobby from the Lord Provost, 1867. Licensed.' The collar is in the Museum of Edinburgh. The faithful terrier was buried in the kirkyard in 1872.

A 60
**Greyfriars Kirkyard**

When the burial ground at St Giles' High Kirk filled up, Mary Queen of Scots, in 1562, allowed the town council to lay out this 'theatre of mortality'. Eroded angels, skeletons and skulls populate the memorials. The monument shown here, dated 1675, with cherubs on the pediment, commemorates an advocate, James Chalmers. Architect William Adam's family mausoleum, designed by his sons Robert and John, can be found; also the grave of James Craig, designer of the New Town Plan.

There is a section of the Flodden Wall, built to protect Edinburgh from an English invasion that was feared after Scottish forces were defeated and King James IV killed at the Battle of Flodden in 1513. Here too is the Martyrs' Monument, dedicated to Covenanters imprisoned in the kirkyard following their capture by royalist forces at the Battle of Bothwell Bridge in 1679.

A 61
**The Mackenzie Mausoleum**
Greyfriars Kirkyard

Covenanters who refused to swear loyalty to Charles II were executed or exiled by King's Advocate George 'Bluidy' Mackenzie whose soul, as Robert Louis Stevenson put it, 'is certainly in hell'.

His uneasy spirit lingers in the

mausoleum he commissioned before he died in 1691. The classical domed rotunda is the most sinister piece of architecture in Edinburgh. Poltergeist reported. Ghost tours advertised.

## A 62
**George Heriot's School**
Lauriston Place

George Heriot was goldsmith to James VI, whom he followed to London in 1603. On his death in 1624, he left money for a 'hospital' (meaning school and orphanage) for 'faitherless bairns'.

A romantic silhouette from any point of view (shown here from Victoria Terrace), the school was planned around a quadrangle by William Wallace, Master Mason to the Scottish Crown. A sculpture of Heriot overlooks the quad. The principal façade (1628) faces the Old Town.

The entrance today is on Lauriston Place, where William Playfair designed the gatehouse (1829). It looks like a miniature of the Scottish Renaissance style school.

## A 63
**National Museum of Scotland**
Chambers Street

The Museum of Scotland designed by Benson & Forsyth (1995–98) and the Royal Museum (Captain Francis Fowke with architect Robert Matheson 1861–66) merged as the National Museum of Scotland in 2006.

Prince Albert laid the foundation stone for the Royal Museum in 1861 (it had been founded in 1854 as the Industrial Museum of Scotland). Classical sculptures high above the entrance symbolise Science, Manufacturing, Engineering, Natural History and Applied Art, while portrait medallions below represent Queen Victoria and Prince Albert, Darwin, Michelangelo, Newton and Watt.

The Venetian façade conceals a cast-iron galleried, timber- and glass-roofed exhibition hall. There is no better example in Edinburgh of the Victorian personality caught between progress and the architecture of antiquity.

The design was influenced by the Crystal Palace at London's Great Exhibition (1851), and the Palais de l'Industrie at the Exposition Universelle in Paris (1855), which engineer Fowke attended as a British representative.

The hall is approached from a vaulted undercroft created during refurbishment (Gareth Hoskins Architects, David Narro Associates engineers 2008–11). The ascent and sudden encounter with Fowke's lofty, luminous space is one of Edinburgh's memorable architectural moments.

There is an internal link to the former Museum of Scotland. Its drum-shaped tower evokes castles from the mists of time. An atrium accesses a labyrinth of Scottish history, layered like the Old Town. The roof garden (panoramic views from here) is planted to represent Scottish natural habitats.

A 64
**Heriot-Watt College**
25 Chambers Street

This started in 1821 as Edinburgh Mechanics' Institute, to give working class men (and later women) technical education. It was the first of its kind in the world. Funded by George Heriot's Trust and the Watt Institution, it became Heriot-Watt College in 1885 and a university in 1966. A statue once here of engineer and inventor James Watt is now at Heriot-Watt's Riccarton Campus.

The French Second Empire style building, complete with classical columns, mansard roofs and decorative ironwork, dates from reconstruction in 1885. The sculpture of a boy with a hammer and anvil high above the entrance symbolises crafts and industry. Since 1990, the building has been part of the Sheriff Court complex.

A 65
**Adam House**
5–6 Chambers Street
*William Kininmonth 1954*

A classical revival essay for the University of Edinburgh, inspired by Robert Adam's Old College. The architect explained that it was an attempt to combine modern construction with traditional proportions. In other words 'postmodernism', two decades before such reinterpretation of the past became fashionable.

The name recalls Adam Square, replaced around 1870 by Chambers Street. On Guthrie Street, near Adam House, a wall panel dated 1887 notes that Walter Scott was born in a house here, in 1771.

A 66
**South Bridge**

South Bridge spans the Cowgate ravine on multiple arches. It looked like a Roman aqueduct until hidden by tenements and shops. Only

the arch above the Cowgate remains exposed. The arches, known as South Bridge Vaults, were workshops and storage for businesses above. The underworld is still there, abandoned and spooky.

South Bridge was built (1785–88) to connect the Old Town with the Old College. North Bridge, begun in 1763, provided a direct link to Leith and the New Town.

A 67
**St Cecilia's Hall**
50 Niddry Street
*Robert Mylne 1763*

Scotland's oldest concert hall was built for the Edinburgh Musical Society and named after the patron saint of musicians. Its oval-shaped concert room was a fashionable venue in the Old Town until South Bridge blighted the neighbourhood. Concert-goers moved

to the Assembly Rooms in the New Town. St Cecilia's became successively a Baptist church, a Freemasons lodge, a school, and a 1930s dance hall. In the 1960s, it was adapted for the University of Edinburgh's collection of historic musical instruments.

Page\Park Architects recently refurbished the building, increasing awareness of the collection and access to it. The parrot and flower patterns on the bronze screen above the entrance were inspired by the decoration on a harpsichord displayed inside.

### A 68
**St Patrick's Church**
5 South Gray's Close
*John Baxter 1771–74*

This was Cowgate Chapel, built for the Scottish Episcopal Church. When the congregation moved to the New Town in 1818 the chapel was sold to the United Presbyterians. The Catholic Church bought it in 1856 to serve Highlanders and Irish who migrated to the city for work and to escape poverty.

Architect Baxter's original design echoed St Martin-in-the-Fields in London until overlaid in 1929 with a grandiose neoclassical façade by Reginald Fairlie. In 2018, a mural *The Ascension of the Lord,* painted over by the Presbyterians, was uncovered for restoration.

### A 69
**Dovecot Studios**
10 Infirmary Street
*Robert Morham, City Architect 1887; Malcolm Fraser Architects 2009*

The studios occupy the former Infirmary Street Baths, the first public baths in the city. When the building was repurposed the pool was drained and floored over, but

the original skylit galleried space, timber roof and Victorian façade were retained. Artists collaborate with weavers to create fine tapestries. Facilities include exhibition space, a shop and café.

The enterprise, inspired by William Morris and the Arts and Crafts movement, was founded by the 4th Marquess of Bute in 1912. The name migrated from Corstorphine Doocot where the studios were first established.

A 70
**Edinburgh Climate Change Institute**
High School Yards
*Malcolm Fraser Architects 2013*

Previously named the Edinburgh Centre for Carbon Innovation, this response to climate anxiety is housed in the former Royal High School building of 1777 and in a purpose-built extension. The latter features cross-laminated timber, one of several types of 'engineered' timber that are sustainable, eco-friendly alternatives to steel and concrete.

The centre is the latest layer of history at High School Yards. Here before the Reformation was Blackfriars Monastery. A section of the Flodden Wall can be seen at the foot of Drummond Street. Walter Scott was a pupil at the Royal High School; the initials 'WS' among the 18th century graffiti on the porch facing Infirmary Street are said to have been scratched by him. After the school moved to Calton Hill in 1829, the building was used as a surgical hospital where University of Edinburgh anatomy classes were held.

A 71
**Old Infirmary Building**
High School Yards
*David Bryce 1848–53*

Designed in French Renaissance style and now the University of Edinburgh School of Geoscience, this was built as the New Surgical Hospital, so-called to distinguish it from the hospital in former High School building.

The separate Royal Infirmary building (William Adam 1740) on Infirmary Street was demolished after the hospital, needing more

space to serve a growing population, moved to Lauriston Place. Adam's gateway was salvaged and re-erected on here on Drummond Street.

A 72
**Drummond House**
5 Drummond Street

Colourful masonry, steeply pitched roofs, crow-stepped gables and an octagonal cupola are fanciful ingredients of this Dutch-flavoured confection built in 1905 as St Patrick's Roman Catholic School. Now flats with parking on the

former playground at the back, the school's original doors, marked 'boys' and 'girls', can still be seen.

The central gable contains a stone-carved medallion showing a teacher and a boy with a book symbolising Education, an image common on Edinburgh School Board buildings of the time.

A 73
**Rutherford's Bar**
3 Drummond Street

The teak wood, stand-alone frontage with a horse's head trade mark on the pediment is a rare relic of late 19th century pub design. The bar opened in 1834 and became a hang-out for students at the University of Edinburgh, among them Arthur Conan Doyle and Robert Louis Stevenson.

RLS later wrote: 'How I hoped (if I did not take to drink) I should possibly write one little book.' The restaurant here was previously called the 'Hispaniola', the name of the schooner on which the hero of Stevenson's adventure story *Treasure Island* sets sail. The interior is decorated with pirate paraphernalia.

A 74
**Festival Theatre**
13-29 Nicolson Street

There have been theatres on this site since the 1820s. The most lavish was the Empire Palace of 1892, an Aladdin's cave of gilded décor until gutted by fire in 1911. It was rebuilt in 1928, became a bingo hall in the 1960s and was restored as a theatre in 1994 with a new stage, fly tower and glazed foyer.

There is of course a ghost, namely illusionist Sigmund Neuberger, stage name 'The Great Lafayette', whose act caused the fire of 1911 in which he perished.

A 75
**Surgeons' Hall and Museum**
Nicolson Street
*William Playfair 1832*

The Royal College of Surgeons of Edinburgh was incorporated in 1505 in the Old Town. In 1697, the surgeons moved to High School Yards and subsequently to this Greek Revival temple to their status. The archive holds records from the 1460s, including architect Playfair's plans for the building.

Among past presidents of the college was surgeon and professor Joseph Bell, whose powers of observation and deduction inspired medical student and later novelist Arthur Conan Doyle's fictional detective Sherlock Holmes.

Holmes would have relished the case of museum curator and anatomy teacher Robert Knox who needed bodies for dissection. William Burke and William Hare supplied them, not by grave-robbing but by murder. Burke was executed for his crimes. His body was dissected by a member of the college and his death mask is among the macabre curiosities here.

A 76
**The Old College**
South Bridge
*Robert Adam 1789–93; William Playfair 1816–27; Robert Rowand Anderson (dome) 1887*

No building symbolises better the University of Edinburgh's role since 1583 in the city's cultural and intellectual life than Robert

# Tour A — HOLYROOD AND THE OLD TOWN

Adam's stupendous set piece on South Bridge.

The six colossal Doric columns on the portico were extracted from Craigleith Quarry. Each weighed nine tons, was nine metres long, and were hauled here by horses. Above them, the architect's name is inscribed on a Roman style panel. Like many architects and artists of the time, Adam visited Italy to study the relics of the classical world. On the dome is the 'Golden Boy' holding the Torch of Knowledge.

The columns flank a vaulted archway leading to a quadrangle with neoclassical façades on all sides. William Playfair was appointed architect after Adam died. On the north side is the Law School; on the south side, the Playfair Library.

George IV called the Signet Library in the Old Town 'the finest drawing room in Europe'. He didn't see Playfair's library (photo, page 15). Marble busts of academics mingle with classical columns in a celebration of books and learning. Beyond the library is the Talbot Rice Gallery of contemporary art. Its Georgian Room was originally the university's Natural History Museum, since relocated to the King's Buildings campus.

Playfair's scheme for the quad was not completed due to lack of funds. Until recently, the space was used as a parking lot. In 2011, Playfair's vision of an uncluttered, perfectly proportioned social space was fulfilled by Simpson & Brown Architects, following an archaeological investigation of the site.

# Tour B
# Calton Hill, Princes Street and the New Town

*The National Monument*
*City Observatory*
*Royal High School*
*St Andrew's House*
*Old Calton Burying Ground*
*Balmoral Hotel*
*Café Royal*
*General Register House*
*Picardy Place*
*Mansfield Traquair Centre*
*National Portrait Gallery*

*Melville Monument*
*Dundas House*
*Forsyth's Building*
*Jenners*
*The Scott Monument*
*St Andrew's Church*
*The Dome*
*The National Gallery*
*Northern Lighthouse Board*
*Charlotte Square . . .*

Opposite: *Jenners, Edinburgh's iconic department store on Princes Street, photographed before it closed in 2020 due to the Covid-19 pandemic. It did not reopen but, in 2022, planning permission was granted for a boutique hotel and retail redevelopment sensitive to the building's Category A-listed architectural heritage.*

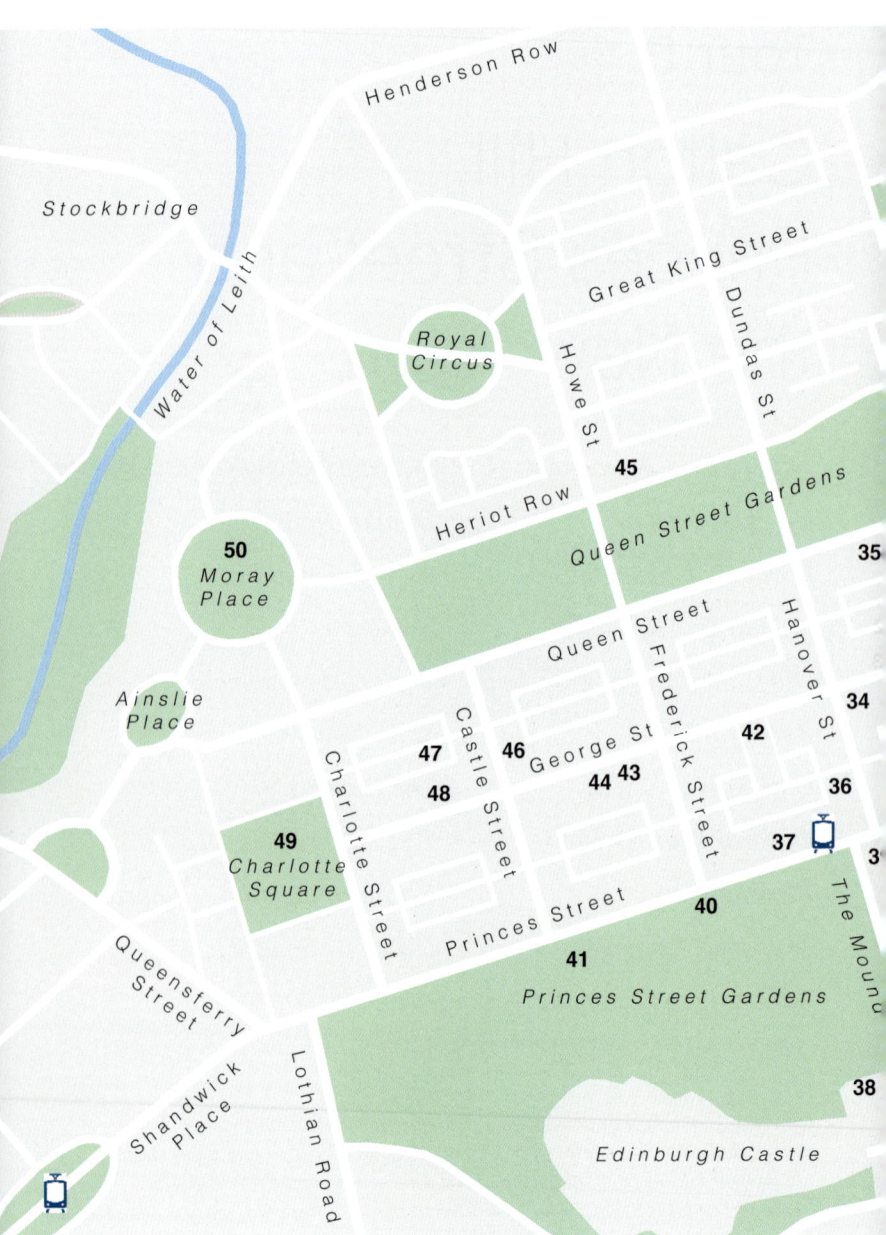

Tour B—**CALTON HILL, PRINCES STREET AND THE NEW TOWN**

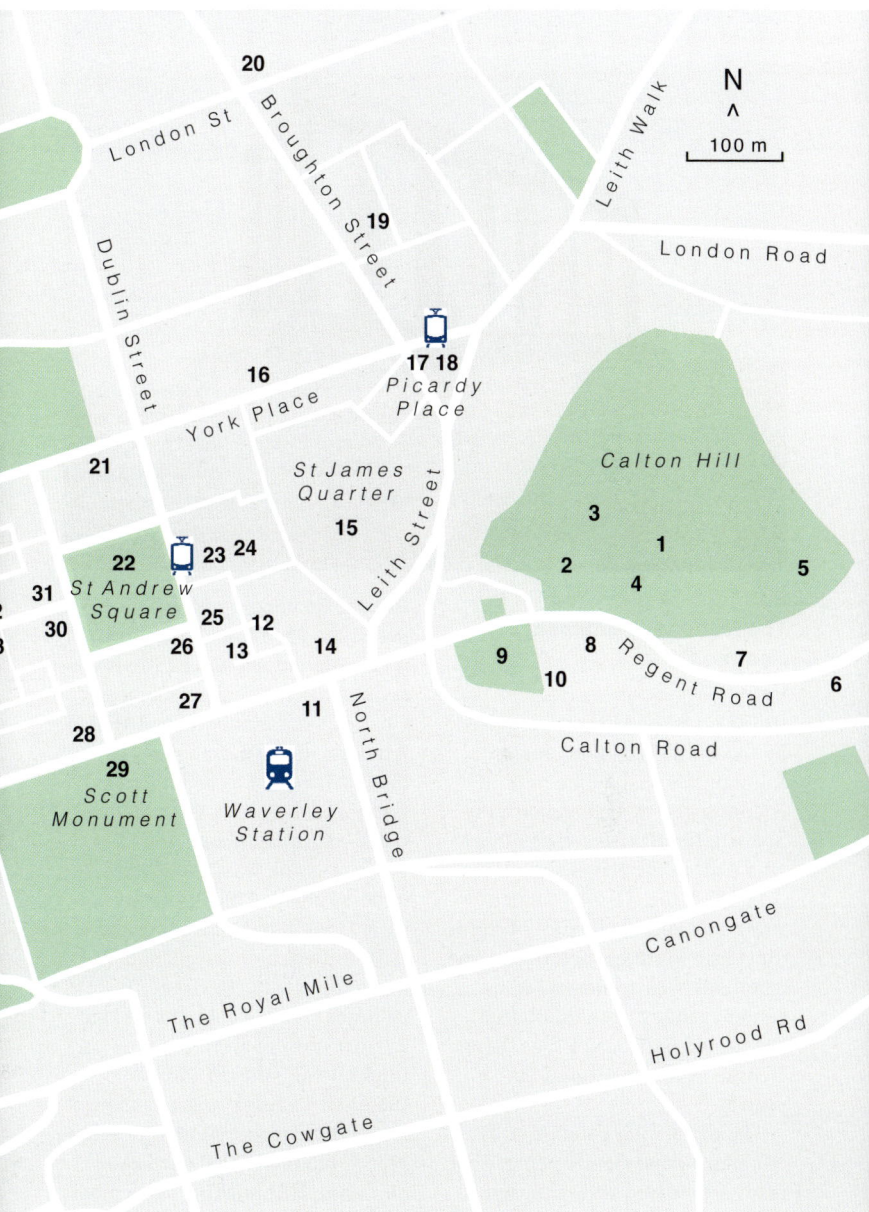

## B 1
**The National Monument of Scotland**
Calton Hill

In 1724, Calton Hill was acquired by the town council to create Edinburgh's first public park. It is dominated by this memorial to Scots in the British armed forces who died in the Napoleonic Wars.

In 1822, the six-ton foundation stone was laid by the Earl of Elgin (of 'Elgin Marbles' notoriety). The ceremony was accompanied by cannon salutes from Edinburgh Castle and Salisbury Crags. King George IV was patron of the project.

The organising committee of 'Noblemen and Gentlemen of Scotland' considered several designs, among them a classical rotunda, like the Pantheon in Rome, proposed for The Mound. Calton Hill was preferred and Greek Revival style. Architect and archaeologist Charles Cockerell, who had visited Athens and made drawings of the Parthenon, was appointed on Elgin's advice, with William Playfair the local architect.

The mission was epic. Teams of horses hauled blocks of stone from Craigleith Quarry to Calton Hill. A great hall was planned, to be wrapped with 46 Greek Doric columns. Twelve columns and an architrave were erected before fund raising faltered and the 'Scottish Valhalla' was abandoned. It was derided as 'Edinburgh's disgrace', but the 'failed Parthenon' on Calton Hill remains *the* symbol of 'The Athens of the North'.

## B 2
**Dugald Stewart Monument**
Calton Hill
*William Playfair 1831*

Another legacy from the 'Athens of the North' is this tribute to philosopher Dugald Stewart. The circular structure with nine Corinthian columns was inspired by the Choragic Monument of Lysicrates in Athens.

Stewart was Professor of Moral Philosophy at the University of Edinburgh and a leading figure of the Scottish Enlightenment. The monument was commissioned by the Royal Society of Edinburgh.

## B 3
**City Observatory**
Calton Hill
*William Playfair 1818*

This elegant temple of celestial enquiry is the centrepiece in a walled compound among the architectural curiosities on top of Calton Hill.

The Playfair Monument (1822) on the compound's southeast corner honours architect William Playfair's uncle, John Playfair, President of the Astronomical Institution for which the observatory was built. The site became the Royal Observatory in 1822, later relocated to Blackford Hill.

On the southwest corner is Old Observatory House (1776), designed by James Craig, where lived Thomas Short who built the first observatory here, of which nothing remains. The house was enlarged in 1883 for Astronomer Royal, Charles Piazzi Smyth.

The northwest corner contains the City Dome (Robert Morham, City Architect 1895) built for a telescope too large to fit Playfair's original building.

The site has been transformed by Collective Architecture (from a plan by Malcolm Fraser Architects) as a new space for the Collective Gallery. The project, completed in 2018, includes a restaurant on the compound's previously empty northwest edge. Conservation of Playfair's observatory (still with a telescope) was aided by the architect's original drawings.

Artworks, food, a 19th-century telescope and panoramic views. Amazing!

### B 4
**Nelson Monument**
Calton Hill
*Robert Burn 1807*

On Trafalgar Day, flags are flown from this telescope-shaped tower erected to commemorate Nelson's famous victory. Traditionally the tower also tells the time. A zinc-clad wooden 'time ball' on a mast was fitted in 1853. Seafarers at Leith harbour could set their chronometers when the ball was raised and dropped at 1.00 pm. When they could see it, that is, depending on the weather. Sound was provided in 1861 by the One o'Clock Gun at the castle.

### B 5
**The Democracy Cairn**
Calton Hill

Sited less prominently than it should be, the cairn commemo-

rates the five-year vigil kept on Regent Road during the campaign for a Scottish parliament. Erected in 1998 by the keepers of the vigil, the poetically inscribed monument is composed of stones from across the nation and a brazier symbolising the flame of freedom.

### B 6
**Burns Monument**
Regent Road
*Thomas Hamilton 1830*

A memorial to Robert Burns, the 'heaven-taught ploughman', elevated here in architecture inspired by

ancient Greece. Thomas Hamilton had previously designed in the same style the Burns Monument (1820) at Alloway, Ayrshire, the bard's birthplace. The marble statue of Burns by sculptor John Flaxman originally inside this rotunda can be seen in the National Portrait Gallery.

B 7
**Royal High School**
Regent Road
*Thomas Hamilton 1825–29*

The school's roots go back to the 12th century when it was the seminary at Holyrood Abbey. Mary Queen of Scots transferred it to the town council in 1566. It was located at High School Yards in the Old Town before being moved to Calton Hill, closer to the New Town. The school relocated to the suburbs in 1968, leaving its landmark Greek Revival building abandoned on the hill.

Ideas for its reuse came and went. The main hall was refurbished in 1979 for a Scottish Assembly that never assembled, and two decades later was considered and dismissed as a home for the new Scottish Parliament. A national museum of photography was proposed, the site being close to Rock House, the former studio of pioneering Victorian photographers Hill and Adamson.

In 2020, a plan to convert and extend the old school as a luxury hotel was rejected as inappropriate by the Scottish Government after a public enquiry. Instead, it will house a National Centre for Music, for which the Royal High School Preservation Trust received planning permission in 2024.

B 8
**St Andrew's House**
Regent Road
*Thomas Tait 1934–39; refurbished 2002 by Reiach & Hall Architects for the Scottish Government*

HM Office of Works in London proposed a no-frills design for this headquarters of the Scottish Office, the British state's agency in Scotland. The Scottish cultural establishment said 'think again'. Even the Palace commented: 'Their Majesties take a great interest in the City of Edinburgh, and they do hope that something noble and worthy of this site may be built.'

The result was this awesome Art Deco effort by London-Scottish architects Burnet, Tait & Lorne. The ornamental programme was assertively Scottish. The pillars

flanking the unicorn and lion rampant on the royal coat of arms at the entrance are decorated with thistles; the floor in the foyer has the Saltire embedded. Statuary on the façade symbolises Education, Fisheries, Agriculture, Health, Statecraft and Architecture. The finely crafted stonework conceals what was then the largest steel-framed building in Europe.

B 9
**Old Calton Burying Ground**
Waterloo Place

The cemetery was established in 1718 by the Incorporated Trades of Calton. A century later it was bisected when Waterloo Place was laid out. The north section (gate on Calton Hill Street) has the oldest gravestone, dedicated in 1720 to a shoemaker. Monuments in the south section reflect wealth and privilege. Ironically, they are dominated by the Political Martyrs' Monument of 1844. The obelisk commemorates five political radicals who were charged in

1793 of sedition and sentenced to be transported to Botany Bay, the penal colony in Australia.

The outstanding architectural design is David Hume's tomb, created by his friend Robert Adam in 1777. The most unexpected memorial is a statue of Abraham Lincoln with a freed slave. It was erected in 1893 in memory of Scottish Americans who fought against the slave-owning Confederates in the American Civil War.

B 10
**Calton Jail Governor's House**
Regent Road
*Archibald Elliot 1817*

Governor's House was part of Calton Jail (1796), once Scotland's biggest prison. Designed by Robert Adam, it was a forbidding Gothic fortress on the side of Calton Hill. 'A piece of undoubted bad taste to give so glorious an eminence to

a prison', was the verdict of Lord Henry Cockburn.

When the jail was demolished to make way for St Andrew's House, Governor's House was saved and refurbished as part of the Scottish Office complex.

B 11
**Balmoral Hotel**
1 Princes Street
*William Hamilton Beattie 1896–1902*

The clock tower has been a landmark at the east end of Princes Street since 1902, the clock traditionally set three minutes fast so travellers headed for Waverley Station won't miss their trains.

The hotel opened as the North British Hotel, the second largest railway hotel in Britain after St Pancras in London. In 1991, it was rebranded The Balmoral, a reference to Queen Victoria's castle in the Highlands.

Waverley Station was constructed in several stages (1846–1902). The name was inspired by the popularity of Walter Scott's 'Waverley' novels. The immense glass roof is supported on steel girders and cast-iron Corinthian columns. At concourse level is the original glass-domed Renaissance-style waiting room.

B 12
**The Café Royal**
19 West Register Street

The 'café' in this Parisian style corner block of 1862 is a classic Victorian 'gin palace'. The interior is stunning with Royal Doulton ceramic tile panels featuring famous inventors.

The panels were exhibited at the International Inventions Exhibition of 1885 in London. The following year, they were displayed at Edinburgh's International Exhibition of Industry, Science and Art. Around 1900, they were installed in the Café Royal Hotel and Oyster

Bar, as it was called (the seafood is advertised with a model lobster outside). The striking stained glass windows, made by the James Ballantine studio, depict sports, a popular decorative theme (archery and deer stalking shown here).

B 13
**Cowan's Warehouse**
38 West Register Street
*William Hamilton Beattie 1864*

A Venetian Gothic fantasy, once

the printing and stationery office of Alex Cowan & Sons. Walter Scott wrote on Cowan-made paper and editions of the 'Waverley' novels were printed on it. The warehouse, decorated with carvings of reptiles, birds, other animals and plants, looks like an illustration from Ruskin's *The Stones of Venice*.

In 2018, the cast-iron and timber structure was torn down. The stone façades, secured to the steel frame of a new office block, were restored and the mansard roof was recreated.

B 14
**National Records of Scotland General Register House**
2 Princes Street
*Robert and James Adam 1774–88*

This was the first archives and public record office in Britain built for the purpose and is one of the oldest in the world still used as intended.

James Craig's New Town Plan anticipated a public building on this site, to punctuate the perspective from North Bridge. The Adam brothers positioned their Palladian façade and dome accordingly. The foundation stone was laid in 1774. Work stopped in 1779 for six years until funding, originally from forfeited Jacobite estates, resumed.

The domed rotunda was inspired by the Pantheon in Rome. The ceiling is decorated with delicate plasterwork typical of the Adam style, the classical theme here

# Tour B — CALTON HILL, PRINCES STREET AND THE NEW TOWN

infiltrated with Scottish thistles. The space was renovated in 2008 for 'ScotlandsPeople Centre' where family histories can be traced.

The bronze statue of the Duke of Wellington, outside since 1852, was designed by Sir John Steell.

### B 15
**St James Quarter**
1 Leith Street

In 1849, Lord Cockburn wrote 'A Letter to the Lord Provost on the Best Ways of Spoiling the Beauty of Edinburgh'. He would be shocked to see the St James Quarter, completed in 2021.

One of Edinburgh's 'best buildings'? The best that can be said is that it replaced the 1960s St James Centre, a 'concrete monstrosity'. The new development – shopping galleria, apartments and a drum-shaped hotel with a curly peak – could be anywhere. The hotel, 'sympathetic to the surrounding World Heritage site and its history' according to its architects, is a pretentious intrusion on the historic skyline.

### B 16
**Raeburn House**
32 York Place

The house (1795) forms part of a terrace typical of the New Town's early development. Its significance is inscribed on a plaque styled as an artist's palette: 'In this house, built by him, Sir Henry Raeburn painted from 1798 to 1809.'

### B 17
**'The Manuscript of Monte Cassino'**
Picardy Place
*Eduardo Paolozzi 1991*

The trio of body parts – a hand, ankle and foot – is a meditation on the displacement of the city's

Italian community branded 'enemy aliens' during the Second World War. Leith-born sculptor Eduardo Paolozzi was one of them. The title of the work refers the Italian monastery of Monte Cassino, known to Paolozzi before it was bombed by Allied aircraft in 1944.

B 18
**Picardy Place**

The name is the only trace of a community of weavers from the Picardie region in France who settled here in the 18th century. The oldest building here now is St Mary's Catholic Cathedral, which evolved from the Chapel of St Mary's whose Gothic façade (1814) by James Gillespie Graham survives. Nearby is St Paul's and St George's Episcopal Church (1818) by Archibald Elliott, built for the congregation previously at Cowgate Chapel.

St Mary's was where, in 1859, the novelist Arthur Conan Doyle was baptised. A statue of his most famous creation, Sherlock Holmes, stands on Picardy Place where Doyle was born in a tenement torn down in 1969 to make way for the traffic roundabout.

B 19
**Richard Murphy House**
2b Hart Street

Architect Richard Murphy once wrote, 'This is a city where many citizens wish that the modern era had never occurred. Modern architecture, it seems to be universally agreed, has spoilt the view.'

On Hart Street there wasn't much of a view to spoil. City council approved Murphy's design after city planners had recommended refusal. The quirky house, completed in 2014, subsequently won several architectural awards.

## B 20
**Mansfield Traquair Centre**
15 Mansfield Place

Nothing outside this Romanesque church designed by Robert Rowand Anderson prepares you for interior, glittering with murals by Phoebe Traquair (photo, page 19). The effect is of illuminated manuscripts come to life in Renaissance and Pre-Raphaelite styles.

In 1998, the century-old church, by then abandoned, was acquired by the Mansfield Traquair Trust to save it from decay. It reopened as an events venue. Restoration of the murals was completed in 2005.

## B 21
**Scottish National Portrait Gallery**
1 Queen Street
*Robert Rowand Anderson 1885–89*

The world's first gallery of its kind was a gift to Scotland from philanthropist and publisher of *The Scotsman*, John Ritchie Findlay, who funded its construction and an endowment. The architecture

was inspired by the Doge's Palace in Venice. The building became a shrine to Scotland's elite and its achievements, much as the Doge's Palace expressed the prestige of the Venetian empire. Curatorial initiatives have since made the gallery's collection of paintings, sculptures and photography socially inclusive.

The façade (photo, page 20) is festooned with statues representing Arts, Science, History, Religion and Industry, sculpted by William Birnie Rhind and others over ten years. On the roof is Clio, muse of History in Greek mythology. The Great Hall has a frieze of characters from Scotland's past, commissioned by Findlay who is present in a portrait unveiled in 1889.

The Victorian interiors were recently restored and upgraded, creating more display space than before (Page\Park Architects 2011). Originally, the gallery was shared with the National Museum of Antiquities. A relic from that period, the Society of Antiquaries Library, was reinstated.

## B 22
**Melville Monument**
St Andrew Square
*William Burn 1821–23*

St Andrew Square is dominated by this colossal monument inspired by Trajan's Column in Rome. On top of it stands the figure of Henry Dundas, 1st Viscount Melville who ruled Scotland for the British state in the late 18th century.

No political appointment could be made without his patronage. He represented an unelected elite opposed to democracy. He was responsible for the exile of radicals, among them those immortalised on the obelisk in Old Calton Burying Ground.

In 1806, he was impeached for misuse of public money while First Lord of the Admiralty, acquitted, but never again held public office. The monument was funded by navy personnel. Engineer Robert Stevenson was consulted to allay fears that the column would fall down.

The most damning charge against Melville is that, to protect economic interests, he delayed the abolition of the transatlantic slave trade to British colonies in the Caribbean. In 2020, following the Black Lives Matter protests, the City of Edinburgh commissioned a plaque 'dedicated to the memory of the more than half-a-million Africans whose enslavement was a consequence of Henry Dundas's actions.'

## B 23
**Dundas House**
36 St Andrew Square
*William Chambers 1772–74*

A handsome Palladian villa built for Lawrence Dundas (cousin to Henry Dundas). James Boswell described him 'a cunning shrewd man of the world'. His shrewdest move was to secure this site, for which James Craig had planned a public building.

In 1795, Dundas House became the Excise Office. The Royal Bank of Scotland bought it in 1825. The Adamesque dining room became the bank's boardroom and the double-height foyer was created. According to a plaque, Craig's New Town Plan was measured from here. Fittingly, his idea for a public building will be fulfilled by the Dunard Centre, currently being built behind Dundas House.

The statue in the forecourt is of Peninsular War hero, politician and one-time governor of the bank, the 4th Earl of Hopetoun, dressed as a Roman imperial consul. His 'virtues' are inscribed on the plinth. In 2020, after a review, a plaque was installed noting not only his achievements but also his association with slavery.

### B 24
**Royal Bank of Scotland Banking Hall**
36 St Andrew Square
*Peddie & Kinnear 1857–61*

Accessed through Dundas House is this stupendous Roman style banking hall. The iron dome, with an oculus inspired by the Pantheon in Rome, is studded with 120 coffered stars. The spandrels contain medallions animated with playful *putti* cast as Agriculture, Arts, Navigation and Commerce.

The hall still serves the bank's customers. Conservation and refurbishment by Michael Laird Architects in 2015 revealed that the original floor was paved with

Minton tiles, some now visible below a panel of toughened glass.

### B 25
**Gleneagles Townhouse**
39 St Andrew Square
*David Bryce 1847-51; 3DReid Architects, Simpson & Brown Architects 2018-22*

The British Linen Company, established in 1746 to grow the Scottish linen industry, was first based at

Tweeddale Court in the Old Town. The company diversified into banking and commissioned this stunning addition to St Andrew Square, modelled on the Palazzo del Capitanio in Vicenza, Italy.

Six free-standing Corinthian columns support statues representing Navigation, Commerce, Manufacturing, Architecture, Science and Agriculture. The interior was conserved during conversion as Gleneagles Townhouse, a members' club and boutique hotel.

B 26
**Prudential Assurance Building**
1–2 St Andrew Square
*Alfred Waterhouse & Son 1895*

On the turreted corner is a statue of Prudence, the public face of the Prudential. Many branches were built in Northern Renaissance style, clad in terracotta and red brick. This was rejected here in favour of stone. The interior was replaced in the 1990s but the Victorian ceramic tile-clad former business hall survives, converted as Tiles café/bar.

B 27
**R W Forsyth Building**
30 Princes Street
*John James Burnet 1907*

Architect J J Burnet visited North America in 1896 and returned with zeal for steel-frame construction, and the challenge of how to sell the new technology to his conservative clients. 'Hide it' was the answer. Forsyth's, the first fully steel-framed building in Scotland, is stone-clad in Edwardian baroque style, embellished with Ionic columns and classical sculptures.

The client was 'Ladies and Gents Outfitter' Robert Wallace Forsyth (for whom Burnet had designed a Parisian style store in Glasgow). An annexe (1925), also by Burnet in baroque style, now luxury apartments, is at 3 St Andrew Square.

The store closed in 1981. On top is the much-loved Forsyth Globe, decorated with *putti* and signs of the zodiac.

## B 28
### Jenners
47–48 Princes Street
*William Hamilton Beattie 1895*

Jenners was named for co-founder Charles Jenner, a linen draper. The first store, 'Kennington and Jenner', established in 1838 in a former townhouse, was destroyed by fire in 1892. From the ashes rose this palace of Victorian consumerism – 'The Most Fashionable Shopping Centre in Scotland', the 'Harrods of the North'.

There were more than 60 departments, lit by electric lights and served by elevators. The interior retains the original 3-storey timber- and glass-roofed, galleried atrium.

Thistles and Charles Jenner's monogram decorate the wrought-iron gates. The façades feature figures of the Four Seasons and caryatids in international costumes. Charles Jenner specified female forms to emphasise that women shoppers sustained his business, now closed (see page 67).

## B 29
### The Scott Monument
Princes Street Gardens
*George Meikle Kemp 1840–46*

No one did more to create the image of Scotland as a romantic land of lochs, mountains, castles and tartan-clad clan chieftains than Sir Walter Scott. He was born in Edinburgh's Old Town in 1771. His 'Waverley' novels were best sellers at home and abroad.

The monument was designed by the self-taught architect George Meikle Kemp who won the competition for it. The flying-buttressed Gothic rocket – 61 metres tall with 287 steps to the top – was inspired by Gothic cathedrals Kemp had seen in France, and by Rosslyn Chapel and Melrose Abbey (which Scott had celebrated in verse).

Some of the competition entries

were classical, appropriate for the 'Athens of the North', but Gothic is closer to the medieval spirit of Scott. Statues represent characters from Scottish history and Scott's novels. The biggest is the writer himself, seated with a book and his deerhound, carved from a single block of Carrara marble by Sir John Steell.

B 30
**Capital Building**
12–13 St Andrew Square

In 1937, the Caledonian Insurance Company, then in a 19th-century building (now the George Hotel), refreshed its image with this new head office commissioned from architects Leslie Grahame Thomson and Frank James Connell.

Alexander Carrick created the bronze figures symbolising 'safety and domestic bliss'. They resemble the work of Norwegian sculptor Gustav Vigeland, which Connell would have seen when visiting Scandinavia in 1934. He returned influenced by modern design he saw there, from which the Capital Building is derived. Carved wooden doors open to reveal the original marble-columned lobby.

B 31
**Standard Life Building**
1 George Street

The Roman numerals below the pediment mark the date (1825) when The Life Insurance Company of Scotland (Standard Life Assurance since 1832) was founded on the Royal Mile. The company moved to its New Town headquarters, designed by David Bryce, in 1839. When the building was reconstructed around 1900, Bryce's pediment was reused.

The sculptural theme of financial planning was appropriated from the parable 'The Wise and Foolish

Virgins' – the foolish are in distress, the wise worry free. The symbolism reappeared in the 1970s on the bronze frieze that decorates the adjoining office building, also for Standard Life.

## B 32
**St Andrew's Church**
13 George Street
*Major Andrew Frazer 1784–87*

This first church in the New Town would have faced St Andrew Square had the site there not been appropriated for Dundas House. The bell tower is decorated with garlands and a ghostly mask of Father Time above the clock. The interior, elliptical in plan, is accessed from a Roman portico.

St Andrew's was where the Reverend Thomas Chalmers led the Disruption of the Church of Scotland in 1843, when rebellious ministers across the nation protested that the people, not the landed gentry, should choose parish ministers. The Disruption was a boon for architects when the dissidents set up their own 'free kirks'.

## B 33
**The Dome**
14 George Street

Designed by David Rhind for the Commercial Bank of Scotland, this 'temple bank', opened in 1847, was later a branch of the Royal Bank of Scotland. The dome in the banking hall inspired the name of the bar and restaurant that opened after RBS moved out in 1993. The sculptural group on the pediment depicts Navigation, Agriculture, Justice, Caledonia (the central figure), Enterprise, Merchandise and Science.

The building was replicated in 1847 as the head office of the Bank of Montreal, the 'Scots' bank in Canada, whose building committee had requested drawings of suitable 'banking houses' from contacts in Scotland.

## B 34
### The Royal Society of Edinburgh
22–26 George Street

Founded in 1783, the society occupies the former Edinburgh Life Assurance Company building (1843) on George Street and the company's subsequent Edwardian baroque headquarters (1909) at Hanover Street. Portraits of the society's past presidents, among them Walter Scott, are displayed inside the George Street building, where the idea of a monument to Scott was first discussed.

Outside is a statue of George IV, commemorating the monarch's visit to Edinburgh in 1822.

## B 35
### Physicians' Hall
9 Queen Street
*Thomas Hamilton 1846*

The Royal College of Physicians was established in 1681 in the Old Town where the physicians funded a free dispensary for the poor, subsidised by treating those who could pay. When those who could pay began to move to the New Town the physicians followed. They hired James Craig in 1775 to design a meeting place, a classical building on George Street which the physicians sold in 1843 to the Commercial Bank of Scotland (whose directors replaced it with what is now The Dome).

The proceeds from the sale funded this Greco-Roman palazzo. Statues represent Hygeia, goddess of health, Asclepius, god of medicine and Hippocrates of the Hippocratic Oath. A garden at the back recalls the Edinburgh Physic Garden, established at Holyrood in 1670 by Robert Sibbald and Andrew Balfour who were among the founders of the college.

## B 36
### The Merchants' Hall
22 Hanover Street

This was the Edinburgh office of the City of Glasgow Bank. The north wing (1866), built first, has a Renaissance-style banking hall. The bank crashed in 1878. Its directors, tried at Edinburgh High Court, were found guilty of fraud.

In 1879, the unfinished palazzo

was bought by the Royal Company of Merchants of the City of Edinburgh. Decorative symbols of its activities were added to the banking hall. The south wing was completed in 1901. In the Secretary and Chamberlain's room, a painting illustrates the receipt of the company's Charter of Incorporation (1681) from Charles II. On the front porch is the merchants' heraldry and motto *Terraque Marique*, 'by land and sea'.

B 37
**The New Club**
86 Princes Street
*Reiach, Hall & Partners 1969*

The club replaced its Victorian Italianate building with this brutalist block, a 'concrete eyesore' according to *The Scotsman*. The most significant feature is a cantilevered walkway above the shops that goes nowhere.

The promenade evolved from the Abercrombie Plan (1949) to make Edinburgh a 'city for tomorrow'. A motorway would have ploughed through the city centre. Princes Street would have been rebuilt with

New Club lookalikes with walkways (intended to separate people from traffic). Some were completed and more heritage buildings were lost before the controversial plan was scrapped in 1982.

B 38
**Goose Pie House**
Ramsay Garden

Nestled high above Princes Street is the former home of poet Allan Ramsay and his artist son, portrait painter Allan Ramsay. Ramsay senior ran a bookshop in the Old Town, near St Giles' Kirk, where in 1725 he opened the city's first circulating library. He was denounced by religious zealots for corrupting folk with 'villainous,

profane and obscene books and plays lent out for an easy price'. His house, Ramsay Lodge (1734), was mocked for a looking like goose pie. In 1893, it was bought by Patrick Geddes and restored as part of Ramsay Garden. A statue of Ramsay is at the foot of The Mound, across from the RSA.

B 39
**Royal Scottish Academy**
The Mound
*William Playfair 1822–26; 1831–36*
**Scottish National Gallery**
*William Playfair 1852*

The Mound is thought to have been created with debris from the Old Town and soil and rock removed from construction sites in the New Town. The earthwork filled what was once part of the Nor' Loch, an artificial lake created in the 15th century for defence below Castle Rock. Picturesque from afar, the loch was polluted with rubbish and effluent from the Old Town. Lord Provost George Drummond ordered it drained in 1759.

William Playfair fashioned the earthwork as a classical landscape on which he sited the Royal Scottish Academy and the Scottish National Gallery to dramatic effect. The Greek Revival RSA building is heavy with fluted Doric columns, Grecian ornament, sphinxes and a stately statue of Queen Victoria (who granted the RSA's charter in 1838).

The neoclassical National Gallery is less ostentatious because

much of the budget for it was spent on engineering, its site being directly above railway tunnels to Waverley Station. The tunnels limit expansion, but recently Hoskins Architects managed to insert a new suite of galleries behind a contemporary façade at the base of the building. The intervention, opened in 2023, is a must-see showcase of Scottish art 1800–1945.

B 40
**Royal Scots Greys Memorial**
West Princes Street Gardens
*William Birnie Rhind 1906*

On a rocky pedestal, this bronze statue of a Scots Greys trooper

# Tour B — CALTON HILL, PRINCES STREET AND THE NEW TOWN

with carbine and wearing the regimental bearskin cap is the most imposing of the military memorials in the gardens. A plaque shows the Scots Grey's famous eagle insignia. Sculptor Birnie Rhind also created the King's Own Scottish Borderers Memorial (1906) on North Bridge and that of Black Watch (1910) at North Bank Street above The Mound.

### B 41
**Wojtek the Soldier Bear**
West Princes Street Gardens

Wojtek, the 'happy warrior' bear, was adopted as an orphaned cub by soldiers of a Polish unit in the Second World War and was their mascot during the Italian Campaign. After the war, Polish army units were demobbed in Scotland where many of their soldiers settled. Wojtek became an attraction at Edinburgh Zoo.

The statues by sculptor Alan Herriot were cast at Powderhall Bronze in Granton and unveiled in 2015.

### B 42
**Assembly Rooms**
54 George Street
*John Henderson 1784–87; William Burn (portico) 1818*

The name comes from Assembly Close where the Old Town's wealthy residents gathered at 'assemblies' to dance and party. When they left for the New Town, the City donated land for this new venue which opened with the beau monde attending the Caledonian Hunt Ball.

For two centuries, social and

cultural gatherings have been held under the crystal galaxy of chandeliers in the ballroom. George IV's attendance in 1822 caused a traffic jam of horse-drawn carriages on George Street. Edinburgh Festival events have been held here since the festival began in 1947.

B 43
**78–80 George Street**
*John James Burnet 1903–07*

Burnet's Glasgow commercial style completely disrupts the Georgian streetscape, but what a way to do it! The façade is a cascade of Ionic columns, baroque pediments, and sculpted figures of the Four Seasons on the Italianate eaves gallery.

The client was the Professional and Civil Service Supply Association, a co-op for white-collar workers. This was its department store. The Scottish Co-operative Wholesale Society took it over in 1936. The interior was gutted for offices in 1972. The columns at the entrance are replicas of those that were removed by the SCWS. The rear elevation in Rose Street North Lane is a remarkably modern grid of glazed white brick and glass to maximise daylight inside.

B 44
**Northern Lighthouse Board**
84 George Street

The façade of 1788 looks as it was in 1832 when the NLB, founded in 1786, opened its headquarters here. Among its employees were Robert Louis Stevenson's father, Thomas Stevenson, and grandfather, Robert Stevenson, both lighthouse engineers. Robert Stevenson was also the engineer of the Melville Monument on St Andrew Square. The model lighthouse above the fanlight window symbolises the NLB's founding purpose: to protect mariners from shipwreck.

## Tour B—CALTON HILL, PRINCES STREET AND THE NEW TOWN

### B 45
**Robert Louis Stevenson House**
17 Heriot Row

The first phase of the New Town was later altered by commercial development. The 'second New Town', north of Queen Street, remains largely intact. Heriot Row, a wide street of early 1800s townhouses, is typical. It was named for George Heriot's Trust whose governors invested in land here.

On the façade at number 17 a stone is inscribed: 'The Home of Robert Louis Stevenson 1857–80'. The last verse of his poem *The Lamplighter* is on a brass plate by the street light where the young Stevenson would have watched the gas lamp being lit.

### B 46
**Walter Scott's Townhouse**
39 North Castle Street

When Scott lived here he arranged the royal visit to Edinburgh in 1822 of George IV, the first reigning British monarch to appear in Scotland since the Act of Union.

The occasion was significant for the royal rehabilitation of tartan which had been banned after the defeat of the Jacobite rising of 1745. Scott sent invitations to clan chieftains to attend the ceremonies in full Highland dress. He flattered George IV, as heir to a noble tradition, to wear the Royal Stuart tartan.

The 'King's Jaunt', as author John Prebble called it, had a lasting effect – every trader selling tartan souvenirs on the Royal Mile today can be grateful for it.

### B 47
**The Oxford Bar**
8 Young Street

Turn any corner in Edinburgh and you're likely to find that a writer has been there before. The

Oxford Bar is associated with the fictional detective John Rebus and his creator, writer Ian Rankin. It is thought to have been a pub since 1811. Originally it was residential, built around 1780 by John Young, the first property developer in the New Town. Where did the 'Ox' get its name? Nobody, not even Rebus, knows for sure.

B 48
**Church of Scotland Offices**
121 George Street
*Sydney Mitchell & Wilson 1911*

'Florentine in feeling' said *The Scotsman*, referring to the building's eaves gallery and arcade; Scandinavian too, in the austere reworking of those Renaissance features.

The façade is asymmetrical due to a 1933 addition after the union in 1929 of the United Free Church and the Church of Scotland. Above the entrance is the coat of arms – angels, the burning bush, the dove of peace and Noah's Ark – and an elaborate escutcheon for flagpoles.

Thomas Chalmers, the founding Moderator of the General Assembly of the Free Church of Scotland, is honoured with a statue erected nearby in 1878, at the intersection of George Street and Castle Street.

B 49
**Charlotte Square**

Originally 'St George's Square' on the New Town Plan, the name was changed in 1785 to 'Charlotte', George III's queen, because there already was a George Square (see D 45).

Charlotte Square is graced with green space, and townhouses designed by Robert Adam. It remains the most elegant example of urban design that evolved from the New Town Plan. The apartments attracted a who's who of aristocratic buyers. 'The Georgian House',

restored by the National Trust for Scotland and furnished in period style, shows how privileged they were.

The bronze equestrian statue in the centre of the square commemorates Prince Albert. The elegiac monument was completed in 1876 after more than a decade of planning and debate. Every detail of the design had to be approved by the widowed Queen Victoria.

The prince is dressed as an honorary field marshal. Narrative panels adorn the granite pedestal. Around it are figurative groups (by several sculptors) of 'society in mourning'. The monument was unveiled by the queen, who knighted the statue's sculptor, John Steell, at Holyroodhouse later that day.

On the west side of the square is the former St George's Church (1811–14). The design was sketched in 1791 by Robert Adam. Four neoclassical cupolas were to have risen at each corner of the structure to frame the dome. The composition was diluted by Adam's successor, Robert Reid, probably to reduce costs. The building, repurposed around 1970 with five floors of offices and storage for the National Records, was renamed West Register House, a satellite of General Register House.

## B 50
### Moray Place
*James Gillespie Graham 1822–36*

The Earl of Moray imposed strict rules on buyers of his feued lots

on the Moray Estate, to conform to the grand plan he commissioned from architect Gillespie Graham.

The architectural climax is this neoclassical circus wrapped with townhouses in the style of Robert Adam. All the features for which Georgian architecture and urban design in the New Town are admired are here: finely cut stonework on façades punctuated with columns and pediments in Greek Revival style; cast-iron lamp posts, railings and anthemion-patterned balconies, sash windows, and main doors with elegant fanlights. Skylit stairwells access spacious apartments decorated originally in Adamesque style.

The streets here remain paved with granite setts. The architecture is saved from monotony by rhythm of the pediments and columns, and the fortuitous lie of the land which slopes gently. The central private garden for residents is an enviable amenity characteristic of the New Town.

# Tour C
# Lothian Road, the West End and Inverleith

*St John's Church*

*Caledonian Hotel*

*St Cuthbert's Church*

*The Usher Hall*

*Edinburgh International Conference Centre*

*Gladstone Monumnet*

*St Mary's Episcopal Cathedral*

*St Mary's Song School*

*Donaldson's School*

*Scottish National Gallery of Modern Art*

*St Andrew's Catholic Church*

*Dean Cemetery*

*Dean Village*

*St Bernard's Well*

*Stockbridge Colonies*

*Royal Botanic Garden*

*Fettes College . . .*

Opposite: *The Ross Fountain was cast in France in 1862 and shipped in pieces to Leith. What Leith's dock workers thought of the dolphins, mermaids, female figures symbolising arts and sciences, and the naked water nymph is not recorded. Dean Ramsay, the minister at St John's Church near where the fountain was assembled in 1872, declared it to be 'grossly indecent and disgusting; insulting and offensive to the moral feelings of the community and disgraceful to the City'.*

# EDINBURGH'S BEST BUILDINGS

## Tour C—LOTHIAN ROAD, THE WEST END AND INVERLEITH

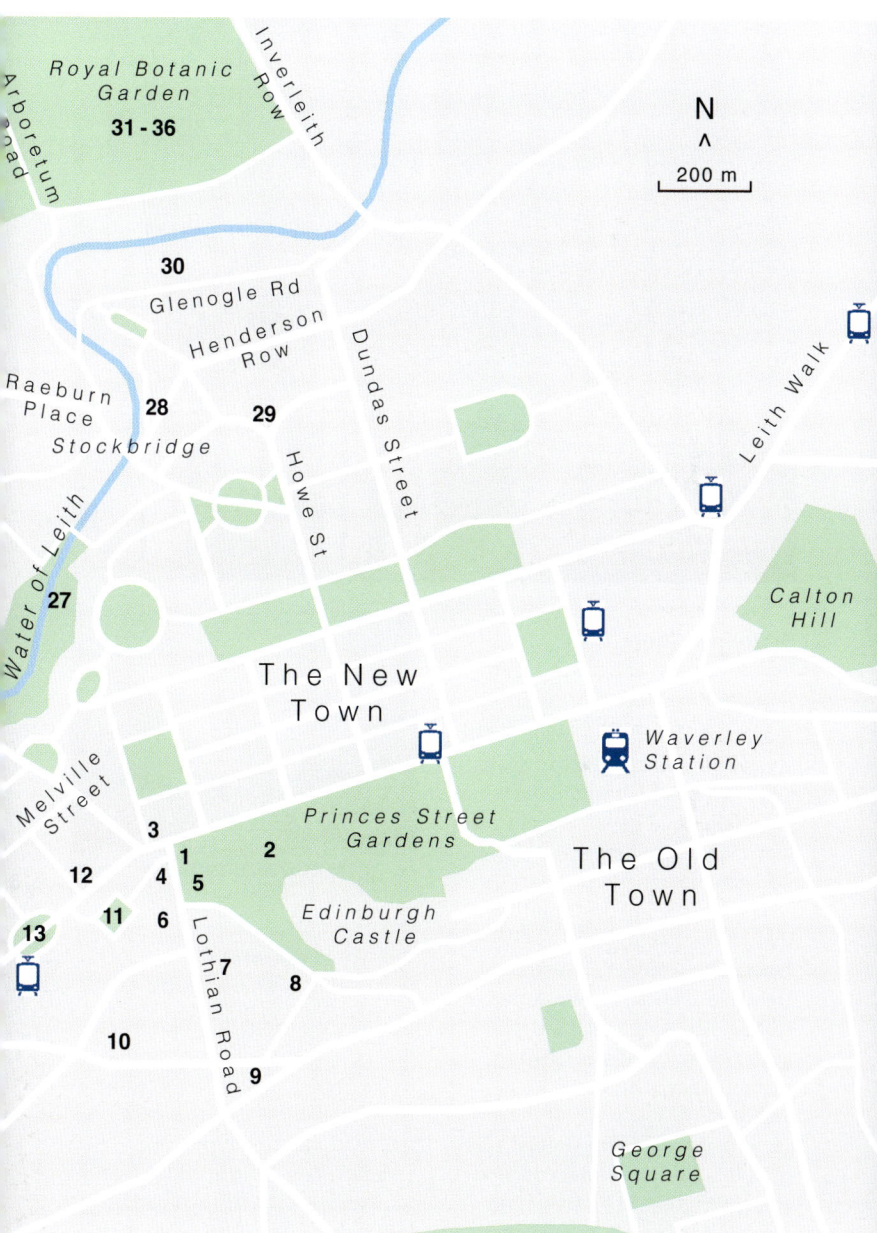

### C 1
**St John's Church**
Princes Street at Lothian Road
*William Burn 1818*

A sermon in Perpendicular Gothic style with pinnacles, buttresses, and a tower which would have been taller had its lantern not collapsed in a gale before the church was completed.

The nave is lined with pillars that bloom like daffodils with fan-vaulting modelled on that of Henry VII's Chapel, Westminster Abbey. Above the altar a triptych glittering with mosaics displays painted figures of Mary, Jesus and St John. The walls of the nave seem to dissolve into stained glass. In 2002, the space was redecorated and brightly lit by Benjamin Tindall Architects.

### C 2
**The Ross Fountain**
West Princes Street Gardens

Daniel Ross from Edinburgh saw this cast-iron fountain exhibited by its French maker, the Antoine Durenne Foundry, at the 1862 International Exhibition in London. Ross bought and gifted it to his home city, whose councillors didn't know what to do with it. Eventually, its 122 pieces were reassembled in Princes Street Gardens despite opposition from Dean Ramsay, the minister at St John's Church (see page 95).

In 2017, the fountain was dismantled piece-by-piece for repair and restoration. It reappeared in 2018, glorious in a 19th-century French colour scheme.

C 3
**Johnnie Walker Princes Street**
145 Princes Street
*J R MacKay 1935; Simpson & Brown Architects 2021*

Whisky galore in an old department store, now a Scotch whisky visitor experience named for the Johnnie Walker brand. It used to be Binns department store, later House of Fraser, closed in 2018. A stone-carved 'B' for 'Binns' can be seen on the façade above the recently restored Binns Clock at the Princes Street and Hope Street corner. The musical timepiece is famed for its hand-painted toy Highlanders, animated to march out twice an hour.

C 4
**The Caledonian Hotel**
Lothian Road at Princes Street
*Kinnear & Peddie 1890–93; J M Dick Peddie & George Washington Browne 1899–1903*

Allegorical figures of Engineering, Agriculture, Commerce and the Arts appear above the entrance to this châteauesque hotel, built by the Caledonian Railway Company. The pediment displays the Caley's coat of arms, flanked by figures representing the railway as a force of speed and progress.

The hotel is clad with red sandstone commonly used in Glasgow where the Caley was based. The hotel was part of Princes Street Station which closed in 1965. The iron and glass train shed was demolished and the rail yards were abandoned, until redeveloped in the 1990s as the Exchange Financial District. The station concourse survives, re-roofed to create an atrium for the hotel, now the Waldorf Astoria. The cast-iron and timber gateway on Rutland Street was restored.

## C 5
**St Cuthbert's Parish Church**
5 Lothian Road

The 'Kirk below the Castle' is on the oldest Christian site in the city where, it is believed, the Celtic missionary St Cuthbert founded a chapel in the 7th century. The present church, an Italianate basilica with two baroque towers (1894) incorporates the 18th-century tower of the previous church here.

By the kirkyard wall on Lothian Road is a miniature castle, actually a watchtower built to deter grave robbers. The 'Resurrectionists', better known as 'body snatchers', dug up corpses and sold them to the University of Edinburgh for anatomy lessons. Graves in many cemeteries were protected with cast-iron railings and heavy stone slabs. The 1832 Anatomy Act regulated the use of corpses for medical training and put the body snatchers out of business.

## C 6
**Standard Life House**
30 Lothian Road
*Michael Laird & Partners 1996*

The company moved its headquarters from the New Town to this building, the first in the Exchange Financial District planned for the City by architects Terry Farrell & Partners. The district's architectural style is postmodern, characterised by superficial references to the past. The domes and stone-clad façades of Standard Life House look to have been inspired by the Beaux-Arts style of the Usher Hall.

## C 7
**The Usher Hall**
Lothian Road
*James Stockdale Harrison and Howard Henry Thomson 1910–14*

The City of Edinburgh's domed concert hall was funded by the beer and whisky tycoon Andrew Usher. George V and Queen Mary laid the foundation stone. Sculptures of female figures on the

façade represent the joy of music (one holds a model of the building).

The façade conceals a reinforced concrete and steel structure. The dome is a stylistic conceit: the auditorium below it is not circular but horseshoe-shaped. In harmony with the radius of the dome is an extension by LDN Architects (2009), fully glazed to make clear what's new and what's old.

### C 8
**Castle Terrace**
*James Gowans 1866–70*

A bizarre block of tenements with crown-shaped turrets, massed ranks of chimneys, hooded gables, and spandrels with Moorish serrated stonework. Beside the corner gable are *putti* representing a mason and an architect (perhaps the eccentric Gowans himself in good humour). Above them is an unidentified classical goddess by William Brodie, best known for the sculpture of Greyfriars Bobby.

### C 9
**St Cuthbert's Co-operative Society**
Bread Street

This former furniture showroom has the first glazed curtain wall attached to a building in Scotland. Interior gone, but when the façade was renovated around 2000 for a hotel the 1930s lettering style was revived to spell 'Conference Centre'. The former Co-op drapery store (1892) is next door and at the east end of the block is a Parisian domed corner (1914), originally St Cuthbert's Emporium.

C 10
**Edinburgh International Conference Centre**
150 Morrison Street
*Terry Farrell & Partners 1995*

With a halo of steelwork illuminated at night, sail-like canopies, and a glazed curtain wall revealing the foyer, this is the most engaging building in the architecturally disappointing Exchange Financial District. Unfortunately, it wasn't built at Festival Square where its drum shape would have echoed that of the Usher Hall (the Sheraton Hotel was already there).

The district became a ghost town during Covid-19 pandemic lockdowns. The Conference Centre was used as a temporary vaccination centre.

C 11
**Rutland Square**

Tucked away at the end of Rutland Street is one of the city's most intimate and best preserved small squares, planned around 1840 by architect Archibald Elliot. Terraces with Ionic-columned porches and original cast-iron railings and light fittings frame the garden planted at the time.

Based here are the Scottish Arts Club, a members' club and art gallery established in 1873 in the West End (at No. 24 Rutland Square since 1894) and the Royal Incorporation of Scottish Architects (No. 15), both with period interiors. The RIAS, the professional association for chartered architects in Scotland, was founded in 1916. It was gifted its Rutland Square property by founder and first president Robert Rowand Anderson whose town house it was.

C 12
**Charlotte Chapel**
58 Shandwick Place
*David Bryce 1869; Robert Rowand Anderson (tower) 1881*

A pile of baroque braggadocio built as St George's Free Church. Bryce had presented his clients with classical, Gothic Revival, and Italian designs. The latter was chosen. The tower, inspired by the campanile of San Giorgio

Maggiore in Venice, had been intended for the University of Edinburgh's Medical School.

The church is now Charlotte Baptist Chapel. 'Charlotte' refers to a previous chapel (1816) on Rose Street, near Charlotte Square.

C 13
**Gladstone Monument**
Coates Crescent
*James Pittendrigh Macgillivray sculptor 1910*

Liberal Member of Parliament for Midlothian and four-time Prime Minister William Ewart Gladstone stands proud on a pedestal with allegorical figures – Eloquence, Faith, Fortitude, History, Measure and Vitality. Two boys hold a laurel wreath; banners quote Homer's *Iliad*. Three birds of prey recall the family name, 'Gledstane' (not thought related to Gladstone's Land in the Old Town).

The monument, unveiled on St Andrew Square in 1917, was relocated here in 1955, the site for which it was designed but not installed because property owners objected to having it in their park.

History caught up with it in 2022 when the Edinburgh Slavery and Colonialism Legacy Review noted Gladstone's family link to the slave trade. William Ewart's father, Leith-born John Gladstone, owned plantations worked by African slaves in the Caribbean.

The trade continued until 1807, when the Abolition of the Slave Trade Act was passed. Ownership of slaves was not abolished until 1833, and then only because the British government agreed to financially compensate not the slaves but their owners. Like many of them, John Gladstone gained a fortune in compensation for his 'loss of property'.

C 14
**St Mary's Episcopal Cathedral**
Palmerston Place

This Gothic Revival masterpiece, built between 1874 and 1917, was funded by sisters Barbara and Mary Walker who had inherited the Walker estate. They requested the cathedral be named in memory of their mother. The design competition for it was won by George Gilbert Scott. The proposals, three from Scottish, three from English architects, were anonymous. Scott was English. His submission had a cheeky nom de plume, 'Auld Lang Syne'.

After he died in 1878, his design, with a central tower soaring above the cruciform plan, was completed by his son, John Oldrid Scott. Scott senior had proposed two additional towers to face Melville Street. The trustees preferred a traditional west front on Palmerston Place, which is where the towers were built 40 years later by Scott's grandson, Charles Oldrid Scott, after funds were raised.

The central tower is 90 metres high which makes St Mary's the tallest building in Edinburgh. The weight of the tower is distributed to pillars, arches and buttresses – a structural solution medieval stone masons would recognise and applaud. They would be amazed by Eduardo Paolozzi's modern stained-glass Millennium Window illuminating the Resurrection Chapel with heavenly light.

C 15
**St Mary's Song School**
St Mary's Cathedral

On the cathedral's north side are four historic buildings: Old Coates House (17th century), Walpole Hall by Robert Lorimer (1933), and the Chapter House (1890) and St Mary's Song School (1885) by J Oldrid Scott; also West End Medical Practice, a new building by Page\Park Architects (2014) respectful of the historic setting. The Song School is wonderful with an interior decorated with glittering murals painted between 1888 and 1892 by Phoebe Traquair.

C 16
**Edinburgh Trades House**
61 Melville Street

Melville Street is the principal axis of the western New Town, developed in the early to mid 19th century by the Walker family whose estate it was. This end-of-terrace house known as 'Ashfield'

has, since 1971, been the home of Edinburgh Trades House and its library, archive and collection of artefacts. The Incorporated Trades of Edinburgh (15 trades: bakers, candlemakers, goldsmiths et al.) was originally based in the Old Town.

C 17
**Donaldson's School**
West Coates
*William Playfair 1842–51*

Designed in the Elizabethan style favoured by the trustees, this was originally Donaldson's Hospital. Like George Heriot's on the edge of the Old Town, 'hospital' meant a charitable institution, usually a school. This one, for orphans and the 'deaf and disadvantaged', was

funded by the bequest of printer and publisher James Donaldson.

The school relocated shortly before the financial crash of 2008. Eventually, a decade later the Playfair building was converted as flats and a crescent of townhouses was built behind it. The green space at the front was preserved.

C 18
**Belford Hostel**
6–8 Douglas Gardens
*Sydney Mitchell & Wilson 1888*

A Gothic drama, originally Dean Free Church, later Belford Church, rising from the steeply sloping corner site. The square-plan tower supports an octagonal belfry braced with flying buttresses and fringed with gargoyles. The arch above the entrance contains a carving of the biblical burning bush.

The church is now a backpackers' hostel with sleeping pods in the nave under the Victorian hammer beam roof.

C 19
**Scottish National Gallery of Modern Art**
75 Belford Road

Modern One opened in 1984 in a former charitable school, John Watson's Institution (1828) designed by William Burn. Modern Two, opened in 1999, was Dean Orphanage (1833) by Thomas Hamilton. They are set in parkland sprinkled with numerous artworks.

Modern One is reflected in *Landform* by Charles Jencks who saw the formal lawn as a blank canvas for a dreamy earth and water feature. Sculptor Antony Gormley created the enigmatic bronze head and shoulders on the path at Belford Road. The gallery's Greek Revival portico glows with Martin Creed's neon message: *Everything is going to be alright*.

The 'wacky and the wonderful'

Modern Two features Eduardo Paolozzi's reassembled studio and *Vulcan*, his gigantic welded steel pop art sculpture of the Roman god (it looms above patrons in the gallery café). The clock above the neoclassical portico was originally part of Netherbow Port in the Old Town.

C 20
**St Andrew's Catholic Church**
77 Belford Road

In the garden of Edge Hill House, (a Victorian villa bought by the diocese as a clergy house) is this Arts and Crafts church made entirely of timber. Thought to have been prefabricated in Austria, it was assembled as a temporary structure in 1902 but was so well made it's still here. The interior is softly lit from aisle and clerestory windows. Wrought-iron pendant lights with the Saltire motif are suspended from the trussed roof.

C 21
**Daniel Stewart's (Stewart's Melville) College**
Queensferry Road
*David Rhind 1849–55*

Perthshire-born Daniel Stewart, came to Edinburgh to seek his fortune. Having made it, he endowed this school for destitute boys, to be managed by the Merchant Company. David Rhind submitted to the trustees three designs: Italianate, Gothic and an elaborate pastiche of Elizabethan and Jacobean styles which was chosen.

The plan featured a courtyard play area, roofed over in 1906 as a gym and assembly hall. The space is now a performing arts centre designed by Simpson & Brown Architects (2007).

C 22
**Dean Cemetery**
Dean Path

A who's who of 19th-century Scots – academics, advocates, artists, architects, explorers and imperial army officers, inventors, physicians and philosophers – frozen in stone. The most ostentatious memorial is the James Buchanan Monument, a *tempietto* like William Playfair's to Dugald Stewart on Calton Hill.

Playfair himself is here, on 'Lords' Row' by the cemetery's west wall. His self-designed neoclassical tomb (1857) is next to the pyramid-shaped Rutherfurd Memorial, also his work (1852).

The cemetery was laid out in 1846 by architect David Cousin who also designed the burial grounds at Warriston (1843; the first of Edinburgh's Victorian 'garden cemeteries') and Newington (1846). Like them, Dean Cemetery is open to the public. The main gate is on Dean Path; another gate is by the parking lot at the National Gallery Modern Two.

C 23
**Dean Village**

Grain milling was recorded as far back as the 12th century in this steep-sided valley (*dene* in old Scots) of the Water of Leith. By the 16th century, around a dozen mills were here. The village was further industrialised in the 19th century with a whisky distillery, tannery, chemical works and slum housing. John Ritchie Findlay, publisher of *The Scotsman,* could see the slum from his townhouse at 3 Rothesay Terrace above the glen. He decided something should be done.

Architect Sydney Mitchell was commissioned to improve the lives of the workers and their families. The model village he designed for them in the 1880s is an architectural idyll, a blend of Arts and Crafts and 17th-century Scottish Renaissance styles.

C 24
**West Mill**
24 Dean Path, Dean Village

The Incorporation of Baxters (bakers), one of the city's trades

guilds, once operated 11 mills along the Water of Leith. This is the only one left. Their wheat sheaf symbol can be seen on the gable.

If you cross the 18th-century bridge by the mill and you will see the Baxters' granary. Above the door is an eroded panel decorated with bakers' utensils, a sheaf of corn, cherubs and an inscription: 'God bless the Baxters of Edinburgh who built this House 1675.' It was converted as flats in the 1970s, as was West Mill.

C 25
**Drumsheugh Baths**
5 Belford Road

Cast-iron screens by the door spell out 'Drumsheugh Swimming and Turkish Baths Company', the old-

est private baths in Edinburgh. The building (1900) is a reconstruction by architect John James Burnet of his 1880s baths, destroyed by fire in 1892. Stairs lead down to a perfect pool, skylit under a timber-framed roof supported by brick arches on cast-iron columns. The baths are across a Water of Leith footbridge from Dean Village.

C 26
**Holy Trinity Church**
1 Dean Bridge

The church was built in 1838 following the opening of Dean Bridge, constructed (1829–31) for a new road to Queensferry and to open up land for development. The bridge was designed by the eminent engineer Thomas Telford. The church, at the north end of the bridge, is a striking Gothic apparition among the Victorian terraced townhouses nearby. The exterior remained unaltered when change of use in 1957 installed, believe it or not, an electricity substation inside.

## C 27
**St Bernard's Well**
Water of Leith, Stockbridge

A mineral well was discovered here in 1760, supposedly by three schoolboys fishing. Advocate Lord Gardenstone beautified it with this rotunda (1789) designed by landscape painter Alexander Nasmyth.

The Pump Room in the podium was decorated with mosaics in 1887 for publisher William Nelson who had bought the site which he donated to the City. The statue on the podium is Hygeia, goddess of health. The well was later closed, the water declared by the public health officer unsafe to drink.

## C 28
**Stockbridge Library**
11 Hamilton Place

A miniature castle of culture with an octagonal corner turret at Dean

Bank Lane and a pedimented entrance on Hamilton Place. The timber-roofed interior contained a recreation hall, library and reading room. It was opened in 1901 by the Lord Provost as Nelson Hall and North Branch Library, named for publisher Thomas Nelson whose bequest funded similar facilities at Fountainbridge and McDonald Road.

## C 29
**St Stephen's Stockbridge**
105 St Stephen Street
*William Playfair 1828*

This classical church with an octagonal 'great hall' and 50-metre high clock tower was designed to

command the view down Howe Street. The site was suitable for a public school to serve the New Town, but the town council chose Calton Hill and built a new Royal High School there. Meanwhile, a private rival to the Royal High, the Edinburgh Academy, appeared on Henderson Row. The town council's revenge, the story goes, was to encourage William Playfair to block the academy from view.

C 30
**Stockbridge Colonies**
Glenogle Road

In 1861, seven enterprising stonemasons founded the Edinburgh Co-operative Building Company to provide affordable housing and avoid exploitation by landlords. Stockbridge Colonies, originally called Glenogle Park, was the first of several similar ECBC projects, all of which survive. The co-op members were artisans (panels on gable ends here show their tools of trade).

The typology – parallel rows of stone-built, slate-roofed terraces with ground floor flats accessed

from one side and upper units reached by external stairs on the other – is unique to Edinburgh and Leith. The arrangement, unlike tenement living, gave each family a garden. The term 'colonies' came from the ECBC's policy of buying and 'colonising' marginal land.

C 31
**John Hope Gateway**
Royal Botanic Garden, Arboretum Road
*Cullinan Studio 2009*

This award-winning centre was named in honour of 18th-century King's Botanist for Scotland and Regius Keeper of the Botanics, John Hope. It is a showcase of sustainable design, announced by the wind turbine on the roof. The primary source of energy is a biomass boiler and solar panels. Rainwater is harvested. Natural light and ventilation flow through the organic structure.

Wood is the big theme, visible throughout. The cross-laminated timber and glulam beamed roof floats on slender steel columns.

The skylit atrium features a timber staircase. The exterior has Scottish larch cladding. An eatery and exhibition space overlook a reflecting pool and biodiverse landscaping. A slate wall defines the path towards Inverleith House, visually linking the Gateway to its historic setting.

C 32
**Inverleith House**
Royal Botanic Garden

In 1820, the City bought part of Inverleith estate for the Botanics, at the time located near Leith Walk where tenements were replacing green space. Inverleith offered an unspoiled landscape, clean air, and Inverleith House (1774) for the garden's Keeper. The setting with a view to the Old Town is unchanged.

C 33
**The Botanic Cottage**
Royal Botanic Garden
*John Adam 1766; Simpson & Brown Architects 2016*

The Botanic Garden is rooted in a medicinal garden founded in 1670 near Holyrood Abbey. In 1676, it was moved to Trinity College Kirk, and to Leith Walk in 1763 where a cottage was built for the head gardener. The cottage was left behind in the 1820s when the Botanics moved to Inverleith. It was re-erected and restored here in 2016 as the centrepiece in the Botanics Demonstration Garden.

C 34
**Front Range Glasshouses**
Royal Botanic Garden
*Ministry of Public Building & Works Scotland 1964–67*

Pure engineering, anticipating the High Tech style of a decade later, this innovation replaced a rusting range of Edwardian glasshouses.

The 128-metre-long structure – high tensile steel and cable-stayed outriggers from which the glass roof is suspended – was a response to the curator Dr Eddie Kemp's desire to eliminate columns and maximise natural light and space for plants inside, where there were two levels with five climatic zones.

C 35
**Temperate Palm House**
Royal Botanic Garden
*Robert Matheson 1856*

Only Glasgow's Kibble Palace rivals this elegant structure as the finest of its type and period in Scotland. The iron and glass roof, supported on cast-iron columns, seems to float above the neoclassical sandstone façades.

Directly east is the Botanics' oldest glasshouse, the iron and glass Tropical Palm House (1834), the largest glasshouse in Britain at the time (the Temperate Palm House remains the tallest of its type). Both buildings, extensively restored along with the Front Range Glasshouses, are part of the Edinburgh Biomes project – to maintain the Botanics as a centre of excellence for plant science, conservation and biodiversity, and adapt to climate change.

C 36
**Modern Alpine House**
Royal Botanic Garden
*Smith Scott Mullan Associates 2013*

This open-sided steel and glass pavilion creates a microclimate that limits the plants' exposure to rain while allowing natural light to penetrate and fresh air to circulate. The built form increases the wind speed below the roof to help simulate the dry mountain-top conditions that suit Alpine plants, which are displayed here in a naturalistic bedding of tufa, a porous rock.

In complete contrast to the delicate Alpine plants – a contrast typical of the extremes of scale and habitat in the Botanics – are the giant redwoods in the John Muir Grove. The name honours John Muir, the Scottish-born explorer, environmentalist and writer whose work led to the foundation the US National Parks.

C 37
**Fettes College**
Inverleith
*David Bryce 1864–70*

William Fettes was a wine and tea merchant, a director of the British Linen Bank and twice Lord Provost. He died at his townhouse at 13 Charlotte Square in 1836 leaving no heirs. His bequest funded this school 'for children of reduced circumstances'.

The building was a fashionable fantasy (photo, page 17), representing nothing but the best for the underprivileged children for whom it was intended and the reputation of its benefactor. The school itself was a charity, but like some of the city's other 'pauper palaces' it is now a bastion of private education.

Fettes is not open to the public. No matter, because it is best seen from Carrington Road. The cast-iron gates display lion and stag heraldry with the motto *Industria*, symbolised by a bee derived from William Fettes' coat of arms.

C 38
**St Cuthbert's Poorhouse**
Western General Hospital

Above the entrance to this French Renaissance-style building is an eroded plaque: 'Erected by the Parochial Board of the Parish of St Cuthbert'; the date (1867), the board's chairman and architects Peddie & Kinnear are also recorded.

Behind the façade, 400 or so inmates were segregated in sections for the 'Very Decent, Decent, Bastardy and Depraved'. The building was requisitioned by the military in 1915 for wounded soldiers. It is now part of the Western General Hospital.

C 39
**Maggie's Centre**
Western General Hospital

Nothing could be further from judgmental Victorian attitudes to health care than the inclusive and informal Maggie's Centres,

where counselling and comfort are provided to people diagnosed with cancer. This was the first, a conversion of a 19th-century stable by Richard Murphy Architects (1996). It was extended in 2001 and 2020 in the same vernacular by Murphy. The landscape design is eco-friendly. The cosy pavilion in the garden was added in 2022.

C 40
**Nuffield Transplantation Surgery Unit**
Western General Hospital
*Peter Womersley 1965–68*

A concrete bunker built exclusively for transplant surgery, said to have been the world's first such facility, designed to specifications from surgeon Michael Woodruff.

The exterior is characteristic of Brutalism – from the French *béton brut* meaning 'raw concrete'. A hierarchy of sculptural forms expressed the separation of functions: sterilisation unit, operating suite, daylit patients' rooms and ventilation. A skywalk connects to other hospital services. The building is now the Western's chemotherapy centre.

C 41
**FetLor Youth Club**
122 Crewe Road South
*James Robertson Architect 2017*

The clubhouse offers activities to help vulnerable young people in north Edinburgh gain confidence and self-esteem. The building, clad with Corten steel panels, was designed to create 'the sense that the members are in a fort where they feel safe and protected.'

The club was formed by the headmasters and former pupils of Fettes and Loretto Schools after the First World War to support the children of wartime comrades from slums in the Old Town.

# Tour D
# The South Side

*Quartermile*

*Royal Infirmary Buildings*

*The Fire Station, Edinburgh College of Art*

*Edinburgh Printmakers*

*King's Theatre*

*Barclay Viewforth Church*

*Merchiston Castle*

*Dominion Cinema*

*The Canny Man's*

*Hermitage of Braid*

*Royal Observatory*

*King's Buildings Campus*

*Reid Memorial Church*

*Royal Commonwealth Pool*

*National Library of Scotland*

*Summerhall*

*Chapel of St Albert the Great*

*University of Edinburgh Library*

*Greyfriars Charteris Centre*

*McEwan Hall*

*Old Medical School . . .*

Opposite: *The David Hume Tower was named in honour of the genius of the Scottish Enlightenment. It is category A-listed by Historic Environment Scotland as a prime example of modernist architecture. In 2020, the University of Edinburgh renamed it '40 George Square' in response to allegations that Hume was a racist.*

   *Among those who criticised the change was historian Sir Tom Devine, who added: 'On the other hand, Hume might be relieved that the David Hume Tower, the ugliest modern building, among several on the central campus, no longer bears his name.'*

# EDINBURGH'S BEST BUILDINGS

## Tour D—THE SOUTH SIDE

## D 1
**Quartermile**
Lauriston Place
*Foster + Partners architects, Arup engineers 2003–2019*

'One of the largest and most comprehensive regeneration schemes in Scotland', Quartermile was rolled out on the old Royal Infirmary site overlooking the Meadows, the park on land reclaimed from Burgh Loch in the 17th and 18th centuries. The masterplan by Foster and Partners recycled many of the Victorian hospital buildings and inserted minimalist apartment and office blocks across the site.

Completion was delayed by the financial crash of 2008. In 2013, the project was marketed in Hong Kong and Singapore, a first for Edinburgh – globalisation, slick and stylish, but respectful of the setting within Edinburgh's World Heritage Site. It is evolving as a mixed-use neighbourhood with workspaces, retail, homes and leisure amenities – a '15-minute city' where everything is a short walk or bike ride away.

## D 2
**Royal Infirmary Buildings**
Lauriston Place
*David Bryce 1870–79*

The plan, with parallel blocks isolated to reduce the spread of infections, was innovative and influential. The Scots Baronial style was less of a novelty. Nevertheless, the Old Surgical Building is a tour de force.

Above the entrance is a plaque with the building's foundation date (1870) and the birth of the original Infirmary (1729) at High School Yards. There are biblical inscriptions: 'I was a stranger and ye took me in; I was sick and ye visited me'; and in Latin, *Ad Sanitatem Gentium. Patet Omnibus* meaning 'Towards the health of the nation, open to everyone'; also a carved swan symbolising purity. The words recall Lord Provost George Drummond whose idea the Infirmary was for rich and poor alike.

The site was sold in 2001 as part of Quartermile. The Royal Infirmary moved to Little France. Conversion of the Old Surgical Building as a hotel was cancelled in 2008. The building and its neighbours were bought by the University of Edinburgh in 2015. The complex has been creatively retrofitted by Bennetts Associates as Edinburgh Futures Institute.

D 3
**The Fire Station**
Edinburgh College of Art
Lauriston Place

Edinburgh was the world's first municipality with a regular fire service, formed in 1824 when the Great Fire destroyed part of the Old Town. The founder was James Braidwood, the first Master of Fire Engines; his motto, 'Aye Ready'.

This building (1900), designed by City Architect Robert Morham, was the Central Fire Station until operations were transferred to Tollcross. Fire appliances were garaged in the Engine Room. Living quarters for the Firemaster and crews were provided. In 2016, the University of Edinburgh bought the building for use by the adjacent Edinburgh College of Art.

D 4

**Tollcross Community Fire Station**
West Tollcross
*Department of Architectural Services Lothian Regional Council*

This Scottish Fire and Rescue Service facility was built in 1986

to replace the old Central Fire Station as a regional control and training centre. The exterior is playful with postmodern forms trendy at the time. The sheet metal artwork attached at the entrance shows firefighters in action.

D 5
**Meat Market Arches**
Fountainbridge

The classical twins complete with bull's head keystones are a memory of Edinburgh Meat Market (1884) and slaughterhouse (1852). The slaughterhouse (now the site of Tollcross Primary School) was relocated in 1910. The Meat Market buildings (later a 1960s nightclub) were torn down in 2008 for an office block. The arches were rebuilt 75 metres west of their previous position. A plaque in the pavement tells the story. The original meatmarket was at Fleshmarket Close in the Old Town.

D 6
**Edinburgh Printmakers**
1 Dundee Street, Fountainbridge
*1894; Page\Park Architects 2018*

This was the head office of the North British Rubber Company, founded in 1856 by two Americans who had arrived in Scotland with a Goodyear patent. They bought and converted Castle Silk Mills (on the north side of the Union Canal) which became the city's largest industrial enterprise. A workforce of 3,000 people made rubber products, notably more than one

million pairs of Wellington boots for troops in the trenches of the First World War. The plant closed in the 1970s. The site was redeveloped for Fountainbridge Brewery, also gone.

The only North British Rubber Co. building left was saved from decay and retrofitted for Edinburgh Printmakers. Heritage features and the industrial patina were kept as part of the continuing narrative of the historic site.

## D 7
**King's Theatre**
2 Leven Street

An Edwardian baroque beauty with a curved pediment, paired classical columns and, at cornice level, the theatrical masks Comedy and Tragedy. Andrew Carnegie laid the foundation stone. The opening show was a pantomime, *Cinderella*.

The auditorium is frothy with rococo plasterwork. A dramatic mural, *All the World's a Stage* by artist/playwright John Byrne, decorates the ceiling.

In 2022, the King's closed for much-needed upgrades by Capital Theatres to create a multi-purpose venue while preserving its belle-époque personality.

## D 8
**Barclay Viewforth Church**
1 Wright's Houses
*Frederick Thomas Pilkington 1864*

The Free Church of Scotland chose this unconventional design after a competition won in 1861 by Pilkington, a 'rogue architect' with a taste for Ruskinian Gothic. Stone angels hover at the doorway. Carvings on the west side – palm fronds, grape vines and the biblical shepherd with sheep – show how elaborate (and costly) a completed sculptural scheme would have

been. Ghost stones look as if the masons stopped work yesterday.

The interior is a theatrical space with galleries, a rose window and a decorated timber roof. The spire was, at 76 metres, the tallest in the city until St Mary's Cathedral was built. Spooky roofscape, a roost for crows or a dragon's lair perhaps. Edinburgh architecture on the wild side.

D 9
### Old Boroughmuir School
Warrender Park Crescent
*John Alexander Carfrae 1904*

Now student accommodation for the University of Edinburgh, this was built as Boroughmuir School. The building was taken over in 1914 by James Gillespie's High School. Novelist Muriel Spark, a pupil from 1923 to 1935, recalled 'large classrooms, and big windows that looked out over the leafy trees, the skies, and the swooping gulls of Bruntsfield Links.' Her classic Edinburgh novel, *The Prime of Miss Jean Brodie*, was inspired by her time here.

D 10
### Eric Liddell Centre
15 Morningside Road

One of four churches at 'Holy Corner', this opened in 1879 as Morningside North Parish Church. The Romanesque style building was repurposed in 1994 by Groves-Raines Architects for a Christian charity. The makeover created a 'building within a building', arranged to allow the outstanding stained glass windows to remain visible. The centre is named after local hero, Olympic athlete Eric Liddell whose story was told in the 1981 film *Chariots of Fire*.

D 11
### John Livingstone Memorial Stone
1 Chamberlain Road

A gateway with a 17th-century scroll leads to a walled enclosure. Inside is a memorial stone inscribed *Mors Patet Hora Latet* meaning 'Death is sure, the hour uncertain.' Illustrating this grim epigram is a winged hourglass, a skull and cross bones and a eulogy

dated 1645, the year of the Great Plague. The eulogy ends: 'No age shall loose his memory.'

The deceased is thought to have been John Livingstone, laird of Greenhill at the Borough Muir. The muir, part of which survives as Bruntsfield Links golf course, was where plague-infected people were banished from the Old Town for isolation and burial in unmarked graves.

D 12
**Merchiston Castle**
Edinburgh Napier University
10 Colinton Road

This 15th-century tower house, built by the Napiers of Merchiston, was besieged in 1572 by forces loyal to Mary Queen of Scots. The door in midair is thought to have opened to a drawbridge on a platform in the courtyard which would have been protected by an outer defensive wall.

Merchiston Castle School was here until relocated to Colinton in 1930. The City bought the castle in 1935, but it was orphaned until the 1960s when it was adopted by Napier Technical College. The college, named after theologian, inventor and mathematician John Napier, once resident here, is now Edinburgh Napier University.

D 13
**'Lammerburn'**
10 Napier Road
*James Gowans 1860*

Gowans studied building design while working for his father's quarry and construction company. In 1885, he was appointed as Edinburgh's Dean of Guild. He designed the lion and unicorn Masons' Memorial Pillars for the International Exhibition of Industry, Science and Art held on the Meadows in 1886. The pillars were intended to test different types of quarried stone and their durability. They still stand, at the

west end of Melville Drive.

As Dean of Guild, Gowans was responsible for building regulations but, perhaps fortunately for Edinburgh, not style. He built the city's scariest villa, Rockville (1858), a 'Chinese Gothic pagoda' neighbours called 'Nightmare Abbey', demolished in 1966. Its gateposts and boundary wall are across the road from Lammerburn. Lammerburn is strange too, like Rockville but less alarming.

D 14
**Church Hill Theatre**
33 Morningside Road
*Hippolyte Blanc 1892*

This was originally Morningside Free Church, an example of

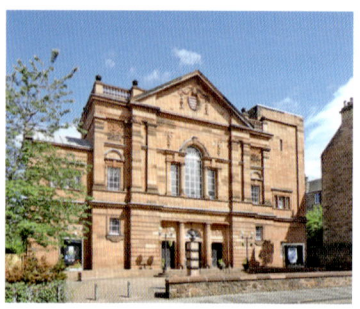

Palladian style, the trademark of the Italian Renaissance architect Andrea Palladio. Church Hill's symmetrical façade, Roman Doric porch, Venetian window, and pediment with an oculus and garlands are defining features.

The building has a base for a bell tower unfortunately not built. It has been a theatre owned by the City since 1965.

D 15
**St Bennets Chapel**
42 Greenhill Gardens

Hard to find a more incongruous sight in Morningside than this Byzantine chapel of 1907 in the garden of a 17th-century style Victorian villa. The house was built for advocate George Seaton. It was bought in 1890 by the Archdiocese of St Andrews and Edinburgh as the archbishop's residence, for which a chapel was required.

The chapel's benefactor was the 3rd Marquess of Bute. The architect, Robert Weir Schultz, a notable Arts and Crafts designer, was Scottish, of German ancestry.

D 16
**Charles Bell Pavilion**
Astley Ainslie Hospital
Whitehouse Terrace

The hospital was established by the Ainslie family bequest in 1900. In 1920, the trustees bought the property here. Patients were admitted in 1923. In 1948, following military use during the Second World War, the hospital became part of the National Health Service.

The Charles Bell Pavilion (1965) was Britain's first rehabilitation unit for convalescing children. It is set in parkland with meadows, mature trees and wildlife. Lost in the landscape is the 16th-century site of St Roque Chapel, named for the patron saint of plague victims. Many were brought here from the Old Town for quarantine and burial in mass graves.

D 17
**St Peter's Church Morningside**
77 Falcon Avenue

Italianate with a campanile as if from a Renaissance painting. The client was Father John Gray who studied for the priesthood at the Scots College in Rome. The

architect was Robert Lorimer. The Romanesque style nave was completed in 1929. An angel in a niche outside holds a model of the clergy house (1907), the first part of the two-stage build.

D 18
**Dominion Cinema**
18 Newbattle Terrace

'Morningside's favourite family owned cinema' is one of the few stand-alone movie theatres still operating. It was designed by Thomas Bowhill Gibson, architect of more than a dozen 'picture palaces'. This one (1938) is the star, with moderne styling, a vertical fin for signage and marquee.

### D 19
**The Canny Man's**
237 Morningside Road

The pub was established in 1871 by James Kerr on the site of an earlier inn patronised by hauliers en route to the city. The original name was The Volunteer's Rest. The local militia drank here after drill and shooting practice (a Victorian rifleman is on the sign).

Inside is a maze of nooks and crannies, overlaid floor to ceiling with the most eccentric collection of bric-a-brac you'll see anywhere. The founder's son was nicknamed 'The Canny Man' meaning shrewd or cautious.

### D 20
**Morningside South Free Church**
15 Braid Road
*Robert Rowand Anderson 1892*

A local landmark by the prolific Anderson, regarded as the leading architect in Scotland of the time. Here, he dramatised the Gothic Revival design with a herringbone-patterned needle spire on a

hefty tower with a slender octagonal stair attached.

One block uphill, in the middle of the road, are the Braid Stones where in the winter of 1815 gallows were raised to execute two highwaymen. The judge directed they be punished not at the Tolbooth jail in the Old Town but at the scene of the crime to where they were made to walk in the snow, followed by a crowd of spectators. The 'Hanging Stanes' mark the last execution in Scotland for highway robbery.

### D 21
**Hermitage of Braid**
69a Braid Road

The trail at the entrance to the Hermitage of Braid and Blackford Hill Local Nature Reserve drops into a wooded glen where Braid burn burbles. On its north side

Tour D—THE SOUTH SIDE

is a doocot like some medieval relic but of no great age. Follow the burn to a meadow and the Hermitage appears as if from a fairy tale.

The name is thought to refer to a hermit here in the 17th century. The first known owner of the land, where deer and wild boar were hunted in the forest, was Henri de Brad, son of a 12th-century Flemish knight. In 1772, nobleman Charles Gordon of Cluny bought the Braid estate and built the Hermitage.

The house, designed by Robert Burn (architect of the Nelson Monument on Calton Hill), was completed around 1785, along with the doocot and a walled garden. In 1937, the property was gifted to the City by owner John McDougal, a Leith grain merchant and opened to the public the following year.

D 22
**The Royal Observatory**
Blackford Hill
*Walter Wood Robertson, Chief Architect to HM Office of Works in Scotland 1892–95*

The observatory was moved from Calton Hill to Blackford Hill where there was space for a new building on a site with clear views of the night sky, far away from Auld Reekie's light pollution and smog.

The two octagonal Italianate towers (the East Tower shown here) each support a metal-framed, copper-clad drum designed to house telescopes which can be pointed at any chosen star. Each drum has a halo of delicate Greek decoration. A sundial on the West Tower is flanked by figures of Dawn and Dusk in bas-relief.

The observatory houses the UK Astronomy Technology Centre and the University of Edinburgh's Institute for Astronomy. The Library collection is renowned. The Visitor Centre offers tours, astronomy lectures and public open nights.

D 23
**Harrison Memorial Arch**
Observatory Road

A triumphal arch, not as might be supposed the gate to the Royal Observatory but a monument to

Lord Provost George Harrison praising his life 'devoted to the public good'. The arch has a plaque recording that during his time in office most of Blackford Hill was acquired and opened as a park in 1884. A bronze portrait of him is set in the pediment.

D 24
**Arcadia Nursery**
University of Edinburgh, King's Buildings Campus
*Malcolm Fraser Architects 2014*

Children of university staff, students and the local community benefit from three eco-friendly pavilions enclosing wooded outdoor play areas. The architecture was programmed around the 'free-play' early learning concept that allows kids to 'learn, play and imagine' in their own way and at their own pace.

The pavilions were constructed with cross-laminated timber made off-site, delivered and bolted together, a process that takes a fraction of the time and labour needed for conventional materials and construction.

D 25
**The Nucleus**
King's Buildings
*Sheppard Robson 2023*

The University of Edinburgh's science and engineering campus was named after George V who laid the foundation stone of the Chemistry Building here in 1920. More buildings, most by Lorimer & Matthew (1924–31), followed as faculties relocated from the Old Town.

The Nucleus, 'the new heart of the King's Buildings campus', provides flexible spaces for learning, teaching and collaboration, and a social commons around an atrium. The idea for it evolved from a 2015 masterplan by Page\Park

Architects and landscape architects HarrisonStevens to stitch together earlier ad hoc development. Public realm design (there wasn't much before) is notable here at Central Green.

D 26
**Noreen and Kenneth Murray Library**
King's Buildings
*Austin-Smith: Lord 2012*

The building boasts a bevy of eco-friendly features and materials – hot water and heating from the on-campus combined heat and energy power plant, internal 'stack effect' natural ventilation, larch timber cladding, Western red cedar louvres for solar shade and a green roof. The internal plan provides acoustically separated spaces for collaborative activity or individual study.

On Central Green, there are two typically muscular artworks by Eduardo Paolozzi.

D 27
**Zoology Building**
King's Buildings

The Zoology block (1928), now known as the Ashworth Building, houses the university's natural history collection, begun in the 17th century at the Old College. On the façades are 14 expressive zoological medallions designed by sculptor Phyllis Bone. They represent creatures from the sub-Arctic, tropical Africa, the Orient, Oceania and South America.

D 28
**Engineering Building**
King's Buildings

In a cartouche high above the entrance is an engineer carved by

Alexander Carrick. He and Phyllis Bone brought artistic prestige to the King's Buildings campus, having worked with Robert Lorimer on sculptures for the National War Memorial at Edinburgh Castle. Carrick also created the figure studying a fossil on the Geology Building nearby.

D 29
**Cameron Toll Shopping Centre**
6 Lady Road
*Michael Laird & Partners 1984*

Modelled on north-American malls, being set in a parking lot with more than 1000 spaces, this was the city's first suburban shopping centre. The conventional design is animated with a sloping wraparound steel and glass canopy. In 2023, to reduce energy costs and the carbon footprint, 330 solar panels were installed on the roof, which hosts four colonies of bees.

D 30
**Suffolk Halls of Residence**
East Suffolk Park

Constructed for the University of Edinburgh these were the first halls of residence purpose-built for female students in Scotland. There are five blocks, built in two phases (1913–17; 1925–28) around a 'village green'. They look like Franco-Scottish country houses of the 17th century but are essentially Edwardian, influenced by the Arts and Crafts architecture of Robert Lorimer.

D 31
**Reid Memorial Church**
West Savile Terrace
*Leslie Grahame Thomson 1929–33*

The architecture is traditional yet somehow timeless. Funds for

it were bequeathed by William Crambe Reid to fulfil the last wish of his father. The tower and lantern are offset from the cruciform plan, composed of a barrel-vaulted nave, chancel and short transepts. The apse, soaring with a monumental trio of stained glass windows portraying the Nativity, Crucifixion and Ascension, steps into a tranquil cloister.

D 32
**Grange House Wyverns**
Grange Loan

Two Victorian gateposts, each with a scary wyvern (a heraldic winged serpent), guarded the carriage drive to Grange House, a baronial pile demolished in 1936. The wyverns were relocated: this one now at Lovers' Loan; the other further along Grange Loan, near Lauder Road, the southeast boundary of the former estate.

D 33
**Mayfield Salisbury Parish Church**
18 West Mayfield

Mayfield Free Church was established in 1875. Hippolyte Blanc was appointed architect after winning a design competition with this characteristic French Gothic design. The tower and steeple were added in 1895. The nave's barrel-vaulted roof is a simplified simulation of the original timber structure which was destroyed by fire in 1969. The rest of the church was spared, including its superb stained glass windows.

'Mayfield Salisbury' dates from 1993 when the declining congregation of Salisbury Church joined Mayfield.

D 34
**Bartholomew House**
12 Duncan Street

This was the head office, studios and print works of the Edinburgh Geographical Institute, better known as map engravers and

publishers John Bartholomew & Son. The complex, opened in 1911, was built by John George Bartholomew, fourth generation in a line of mapmakers from 1797 and a founder of the Royal Scottish Geographical Society.

The classical early 19th-century portico (by Thomas Hamilton) was salvaged from the demolition in 1909 of Falcon Hall in Morningside where Bartholomew and his family lived from 1899 to 1907. Bartholomew House is now flats.

D 35
**Arthur Lodge**
Blacket Place, 60 Dalkeith Road

Arthur Lodge is attributed to Thomas Hamilton, his Greek Revival style here downsized to domestic scale. It was conceived around 1830 by Robert Mason, a builder who promptly went bankrupt. City Treasurer, David Cunningham (who had commissioned Hamilton for the Royal High School), stepped in and bought it.

It was known as 'Salisbury Cottage', Salisbury Crags being nearby, as is Arthur's Seat. The name 'Arthur Lodge' is thought to refer to Major James Arthur who bought the villa in 1841.

It stands on the eastern edge of the Blacket Estate, Edinburgh's first 'garden suburb', planned in the 1820s by James Gillespie Graham. Original gate posts can be seen on Dalkeith Road. The gates were closed at night for security.

D 36
**Royal Commonwealth Pool**
21 Dalkeith Road
*Robert Matthew, Johnson-Marshall & Partners, Arup engineers 1967–70*

The emphatic horizontal form of this City-owned aquatic centre is

deceptive. Step inside and you are embraced by a luminous, virtually column-free space, epic in scale.

The centre was built for the 1970 Commonwealth Games. The event returned to Edinburgh in 1986 (also the diving competitions during the 2014 Commonwealth Games hosted by Glasgow). An extensive renewal of this masterpiece of 20th-century Scottish modernism was completed in 2012.

### D 37
**Scottish Widows Building**
15 Dalkeith Road
*Basil Spence, Glover & Ferguson*
*1976*

The life insurance and pensions company was established in 1815 by 'eminent Scotsmen' in the Royal Exchange Coffee Rooms in the Old Town. The founding purpose was to care for women and children whose menfolk had been killed in the Napoleonic Wars.

Until recently, this iconic piece of architecture on Dalkeith Road was the company's headquarters. The glass-walled, reinforced concrete structure, partly on *pilotis* over a landscaped water feature, was composed of 12 interlocking, open-plan hexagonal pods. The shape of the pods was inspired by the geological structure of basalt, the local volcanic rock. To preserve views of Arthur's Seat and Holyrood Park the complex was kept low. Scottish Widows relocated in 2020, leaving the buildings and the landscaped setting vulnerable to redevelopment.

### D 38
**National Library of Scotland**
33 Salisbury Place
*Andrew Merrylees Associates*
*1988; 1994*

Towering like a modern cathedral, this was built in two stages to augment the National Library's facilities in the Old Town. The glazed grid pattern, internal partitions and floor panels were based on a 90-cm module designed for the bookshelves. The structure descends two and a half floors underground. Cartographic items can be consulted in the Maps Reading Room. The Bartholomew Archive is held here.

### D 39
**Southern Motors Filling Station**
39 Causewayside
*Basil Spence 1933*

This is the city's best example of the Bauhaus-inspired International Style. The steel frame clad in white-rendered concrete integrates vertical fins for signage that retains the original Art Deco font. Offices were cantilevered above the forecourt where motorists pulled in for petrol. A different liquid today: the building is a wine store.

### D 40
**St Peter's Episcopal Church**
14 Lutton Place

The medieval style here was praised in *The Builder* magazine as 'the most complete Gothic church in Edinburgh'. The spire is patterned with cinquefoils. 'Scotch' granite pillars parade in the arcaded nave where the walls and the timber roof were richly coloured with stencil work.

Misguided 'modernisation' in the 1930s saw the original 1860s interior decoration over-painted. In 2009, Benjamin Tindall Architects re-imagined and reinstated it,

inspired by a Victorian engraving and physical evidence.

### D 41
**Summerhall**
1 Summerhall Place

This was the University of Edinburgh's Royal (Dick) School of Veterinary Studies, founded in 1823 by veterinarian William Dick. Completion of its Edwardian baroque building was delayed by the First World War when construction workers here, as elsewhere, joined the armed forces.

After the school relocated in

2010, the site became Summerhall arts centre. The anatomy lecture theatre and other original features in the old building have been preserved. The adjacent Techcube, a 1970s brutalist tower previously the 'Dick Vet' laboratory block, houses start-ups and co-working spaces. There is a craft brewery reviving a tradition – in the 18th century Summerhall Brewery was here. In 2024, the whole site was listed for sale. Hopefully, the arts community will be able to stay.

D 42
**Royal Hospital for Sick Children**
9 Sciennes Road
*George Washington Browne 1895*

Founded in 1860, the hospital was the first in Scotland specially for children. Its first home was a house with eight beds in Lauriston Lane. The second, nearby, was vacated after an outbreak of typhoid in 1890. It was sold to the Royal Infirmary and property on Sciennes Road purchased. On it was erected this Dutch-gabled Jacobean-style building, notable for murals by Phoebe Traquair in its Mortuary Chapel.

In 2019, planning permission for residential conversion was given, following the decision to relocate the 'sick kids' hospital to the Royal Infirmary complex at Little France.

D 43
**Archers Hall**
Buccleuch Street
*Alexander Laing 1776; A F Balfour Paul & Robert Rowand Anderson 1900*

Home of the Royal Company of Archers, formed in 1676 as the sovereign's ceremonial bodyguard in Scotland. The Venetian window and elaborate entrance date from 1900 when the 18th-century building was extended. Above the door is an armorial sculpture featuring archers and the motto in Latin: *Arcu atque animo* meaning 'With bow and spirit.'

D 44
**Chapel of St Albert the Great**
George Square Lane
*Simpson & Brown Architects 2012*

A serene sacred space hidden in the lane at the back of the

Dominican Priory at 24 George Square. Clerestory windows illuminate the interior's envelope of stone and thinly striated oak. The roof above the altar is supported by a quartet of Corten steel columns that splay like the mature sycamore tree outside, connecting the space, through its glazed chancel, with nature in the garden.

### D 45
**Main Library University of Edinburgh**
George Square
*Basil Spence, Glover & Ferguson 1965–67*

George Square, planned in 1766 by architect James Brown, was the first significant development outside the old city walls. The name refers to Brown's older brother, not to King George III. In the 1960s, the square was redeveloped from plans by Basil Spence and Robert Matthew (the university's first Professor of Architecture). Only the Georgian townhouses on the west side, where Walter Scott was raised at number 25, half of the east side and the gardens were spared.

Several monumental brutalist buildings appeared – notably the David Hume Tower (see page 117), the Lecture Theatre and the Main Library. The library, a layered, almost geological slab, was located at the Meadows to the south, the quietest site in the redevelopment zone.

Controversial then as now, the buildings embodied faith in the future. They also contain embodied carbon. Rather than being replaced by carbon-intensive new construction, they have been given energy-efficient upgrades. The most sustainable buildings are those you already have.

### D 46
**Gordon Aikman Lecture Theatre**
George Square
*Robert Matthew, Johnson-Marshall & Partners 1965–70*

Formerly George Square Theatre, this is the most brutal, critics would say, of the new buildings notorious for intruding on historic

George Square in the 1960s. The giant cantilevered box is visually expressive of the raked 481-seat auditorium. Set on a concrete podium, it looms over Buccleuch Place. The entrance is on George Square where the box is equally uncompromising.

D 47
**Potterrow Project University of Edinburgh**
*Bennetts Associates architects, Buro Happold engineers 2005–2018*

The site was cleared in the 1960s but lay empty until a design competition, won by Bennetts Associates with Reiach & Hall Architects, kick-started new construction. The scheme was initially for one building. Bennetts delivered the three-part project: the Informatics Forum, the Dugald Stewart Building and the Bayes Centre. Circulation is focused around skylit atriums with exposed structural steelwork and helical stairs. The buildings enclose a courtyard, reinstating a historic pedestrian route between Bristo Square and Potterrow.

D 48
**Central Mosque and Islamic Centre**
50 Potterrow
*Basil Al Bayati 1988–98*

Islam meets Scots Baronial in this marriage of towers inspired by those at Holyrood Palace and an Islamic arched entrance and minaret. The mosque, one of the largest in Scotland, has a prayer hall built to accommodate 1,200 worshippers.

### D 49
**Greyfriars Charteris Centre**
138–140 Pleasance
*Konishi Gaffney Architects.2022*

This branch of the social enterprise programme rooted at Greyfriars Kirk is based in the old Charteris Memorial Church (1912). With its Scots Baronial tower a local landmark, the church has been revitalised as a community hub, indicated by a stylish new entrance. Interior spaces are energy-efficient and multifunctional. Timber used throughout adds texture, warmth and a feeling of wellbeing, and natural light flows in through the west-facing Gothic window.

### D 50
**Teviot Row House**
University of Edinburgh, Bristo Square

Basking in Scots Baronial style, Teviot Row House, designed by architects Sydney Mitchell & Wilson, opened in 1889. It is the world's oldest custom-built student union building – and a famed

Edinburgh Festival Fringe venue. The outstanding architectural feature is the pair of châteauesque stair towers copied from the 16th-century twins at Falkland Palace, Fife.

### D 51
**McEwan Hall**
Bristo Square
*Robert Rowand Anderson 1887–97*

The Renaissance style McEwan Hall is University of Edinburgh's most palatial building. The concert and graduation hall was funded by brewery baron William McEwan. The design evolved from architect Anderson's scheme for the nearby Medical School, which was built first; the hall ten years later due to lack of funding until McEwan stepped up.

In 2017, the hall reopened after a three-year refurbishment by LDN Architects who designed the new entrance – a circular pod complementing the curve of the 1890s façade. A tunnel connects with the hall's circulation corridor. A short ascent reveals the awe-inspiring auditorium (photo, page 18).

McEwan Hall is now multipurpose. Its original function is seen in the tympanum above the old entrance where a tableau depicts a graduation ceremony.

## D 52
**Old Medical School**
Teviot Place
*Robert Rowand Anderson 1876–86*

The Faculty of Medicine, the oldest in Britain, was founded in 1726, modelled on the medical schools at Padua in Italy and Leiden in the Netherlands. Originally it was at High School Yards in the Old Town. By the mid 19th century, more space was needed and an architectural competition was held.

R R Anderson won it after making 'a whirlwind study tour' visiting medical schools and lecture theatres in the Netherlands, Germany, France and England. His Venetian Renaissance design included a campanile and a graduation hall. The tower was not built here (see entry C 12) but the hall was, eventually, redesigned as McEwan Hall. The Medical School's barrel-vaulted entrance leads to the original Lecture Theatre, and the Anatomical Museum established in 1884.

# Tour E
# Newhaven and Leith

*Newhaven Harbour*

*Starbank House*

*Edinburgh Sculpture Workshop*

*Leith Fort*

*North Leith Parish Church*

*Leith Library and Theatre*

*Leith History Mural*

*Leith Provident Co-operative Society*

*Cables Wynd House*

*Raimes Clark & Co.*

*Cable Tramway Wheels*

*South Leith Parish Church*

*Trinity House*

*Robert Burns statue*

*St Ninian's Church and Manse*

*Leith Custom House*

*King's Wark*

*The Ship on The Shore*

*Malmaison Hotel*

*Port of Leith Distillery . . .*

Opposite: *Lamb's House was named after 16th-century Leith merchant Andro Lamb, who received Mary Queen of Scots at his house when she returned to Scotland from France in 1561. It is not known if this was the spot. The house here today was built by members of Lamb's family in 1610. It is one the finest of its type and period in Scotland.*

# EDINBURGH'S BEST BUILDINGS

## Tour E—NEWHAVEN AND LEITH

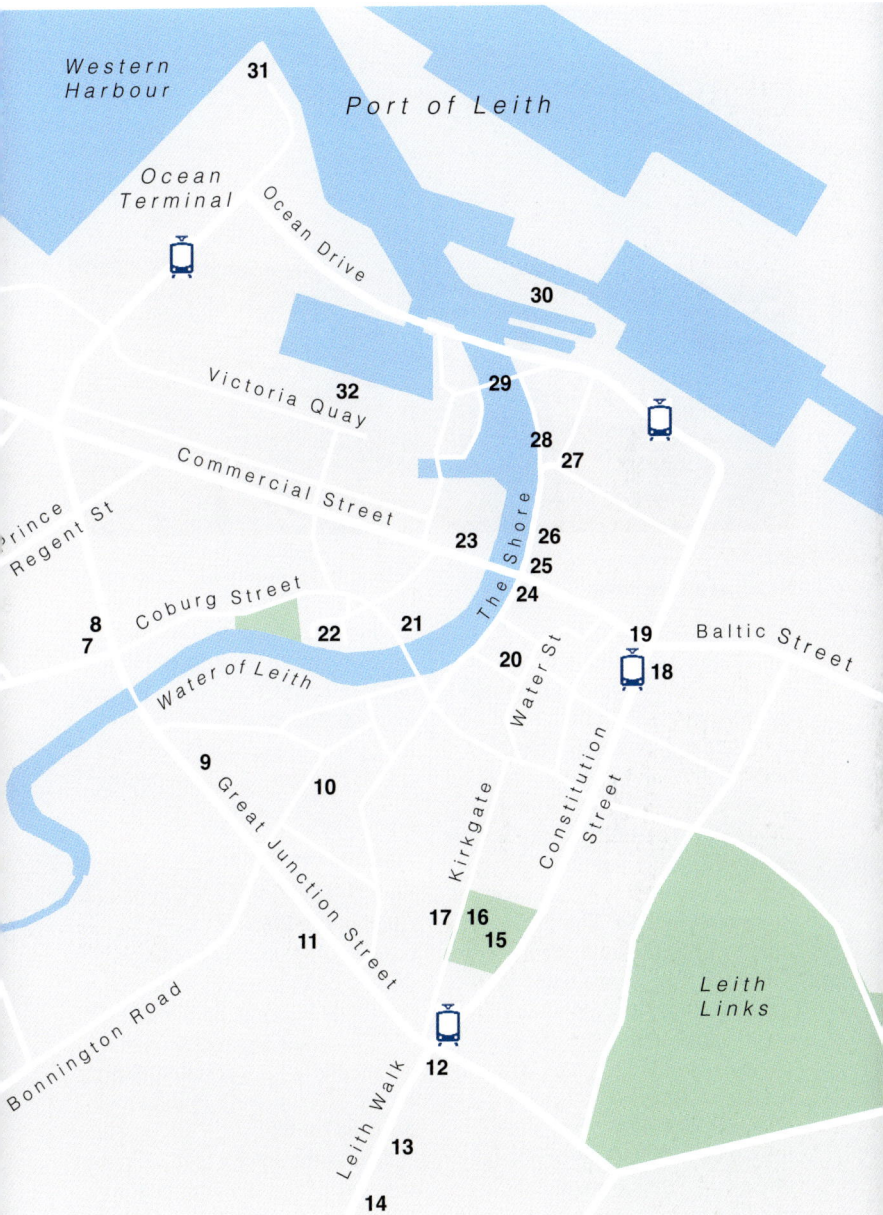

## E 1
### Newhaven Harbour

Newhaven was settled in the 15th century by fisher folk crowded out of Leith, the seaport of Edinburgh. In 1504, James IV built a royal dockyard at Newhaven where his flagship *The Great Michael* was launched in 1511. The harbour was enlarged in the 19th century with a ferry slip (1812) and the breakwater constructed by engineer Robert Stevenson in 1864. The cast-iron lighthouse dates from 1869.

Fishing was the mainstay of the economy. The community was documented in the 1840s by pioneering photographers Hill and Adamson. Images by them in the National Portrait Gallery show fishwives with baskets of herring for sale in Edinburgh, and their menfolk mending nets by beached fishing boats where the coast road is now.

Newhaven Harbour was never a serious rival to the Port of Leith, or Granton Harbour which opened in 1838. The plentiful fishery is long gone, but the Old Fish Market (1896) remains on the east quay.

## E 2
### Fishmarket Square

Most of old Newhaven was demolished in the 1960s. Council houses replaced 18th-century cottages dismissed as slums. The best of the 1960s housing, on the east side of Fishmarket Square, revived the vernacular with forestairs, harling on the exterior walls, gables and pantiled roofs.

Across the square is the Harbour Inn, one of the few 18th-century buildings left. Its gable-end faces

the sea, an orientation typical of the east coast to protect homes from fierce weather.

E 3
**Starbank House**
Starbank Park
17 Laverockbank Road

This wide-eaved Georgian house with a 'Gothick' fanlight above the front door was built around 1815 for a Leith shipbuilder. Leith town council bought the property in 1890 and opened the grounds, now part Edinburgh Parks Department, to the public. The pyramid-roofed bothy is Victorian. The park keeper lived in the house.

The Friends of Starbank Park look after the park, which has a breathtaking view of the sea. 'Starbank' is thought to refer to white stones once laid on the slope below the house to form a star like a ship's compass, since replicated as a star-shaped flower arrangement.

E 4
**Edinburgh Sculpture Workshop**
21 Hawthornvale
*Sutherland Hussey Harris Architects 2012; 2014*

Functional yet stylish spaces built in two phases: the Bill Scott Sculpture Centre followed by the Creative Laboratories. The first is a robust concrete-floored, steel-framed structure with workshops and artists' studios. The second is softer, for research, exhibits and community engagement, with a café facing a courtyard. The centre, built on a disused railway yard, is flagged by a campanile, illuminated at night.

## E 5
**Leith Fort**
North Fort Street
*James Craig 1780*

The fort was built to defend Leith after John Paul Jones, the Scottish-born 'father' of the US Navy, led three warships into the Firth of Forth in 1779 during the American War of Independence. He planned to capture and hold the burgh to ransom, but a storm sabotaged the raid and he sailed away.

The fort, an army base until 1956, was redeveloped with council housing. The council blocks were demolished in 2012 and replaced by Port of Leith Housing Association with homes inspired by the Victorian 'colonies' concept. James Craig's guardhouses, gateway and stone walls still stand on North Fort Street.

## E 6
**North Leith Parish Church**
51 Madeira Street

In 1816, architect William Burn positioned this Greek Revival church to command the view from Prince Regent Street. The building superseded St Ninian's Church which had become too small for the growing congregation of North Leith Parish. The tiered clock tower is a crescendo of classical columns rising to a fluted needle spire and holy cross.

The church was damaged during an air raid on Leith Docks in 1941. Leith Library and Theatre were also hit by German bombing.

## E 7
**Leith Library and Theatre**
28–30 Ferry Road

A plaque in the theatre's foyer commemorates the opening of 'Leith Town Hall and Library' by the Lord Provost of Edinburgh in 1932. The civic centre was built for Leith 'as a gift from the people of Edinburgh' following the Burgh of Leith's reluctant incorporation into the City of Edinburgh in 1920.

The theatre became a legendary performance venue until closed in 1988. In 2004, the City chose to sell it for residential development. Community pushback and the formation of Leith Theatre Trust

## Tour E—NEWHAVEN AND LEITH

have kept it in public ownership. 'Persevere' is Leith's motto and that is what the Trust is doing to restore the building.

The civic centre was designed in classical style by English architects Bradshaw Gass & Hope. The entrance to the library displays Edinburgh's coat of arms above Roman Doric columns that frame the revolving door first opened for the Lord Provost in 1932.

### E 8
**Leith History Mural**
North Junction Street

A narrative of Leith before it was gentrified, painted on a tenement gable-end in 1986 and currently fading like the old Leith it evokes. Industries, political protest and community life are shown in a montage by artists Tim Chalk and Paul Grime.

### E 9
**Leith Provident Co-operative Society**
170–174 Great Junction Street

The 'Provi', once Leith's biggest retailer, built this grandiose tenement in 1911. The store was on the ground floor, surmounted by flats and a domed clock tower. On the façades are symbols of the co-operative movement and its ethos: a beehive, clasped hands and the motto 'Union is Strength'. Leith Provident, founded in 1878, merged in 1975 with St Cuthbert's Co-op (Scotmid since 1981, still based in Edinburgh).

### E 10
**Cables Wynd House**
Cables Wynd

A brutalist slab block typical of 1960s mass housing but with a

bendy bit, hence its nickname 'The Banana Flats'. It was part of a post-war social housing programme that transformed much of urban Scotland, influenced by Le Corbusier's Unite d'Habitation in Marseilles.

Cables Wynd featured in Irvine Welsh's punk novel *Trainspotting*. In 2017, it was Grade A-listed by Historic Environment Scotland for its architectural, social and cultural significance.

E 11
**Dr Bell's School**
101 Great Junction Street

A statue of Andrew Bell, an educational innovator who endowed the school, is set in a niche flanked by narrative panels on the Tudor style façade (c. 1839). Leith School Board acquired the building from Bell's Trust in 1892 and renamed it Great Junction Street School. An annexe on Junction Place and a swimming pool on Great Junction Street were added in the 1890s. The pool, closed two decades ago, is now an events venue.

Victoria Baths, which opened in 1899 on Junction Place, is still in use. The pediment above the double-arched entrance has a finely carved Leith coat of arms: a sailing ship, the Virgin and Child and the motto 'Persevere'.

E 12
**Leith Central Station**
3–23 Leith Walk

Italianate, with an elegant curved corner and clock tower, built by the North British Railway Company as

part of Central Station, opened in 1903. The station was abandoned in the 1970s and demolished. The location inspired a scene in and the title of the novel *Trainspotting*. For travellers' refreshment there was the Central Bar (7–9 Leith Walk), still trading. Superb vintage interior.

### E 13
**Raimes Clark & Co.**
19 Smith's Place

This Palladian villa is the focal point of Smith's Place, a cul-de-sac laid out in 1814 by merchant James Smith, who built the house and the two terraces that frame it. He thought the New Town would extend down Leith Walk. It didn't.

In 1834, the property was sold by Smith's creditors to manufacturing and wholesale chemists, brothers John and Richard Raimes of Raimes Clark & Co. (now Lindsay & Gilmour Pharmacies).

John Raimes started trading in 1816 in the Old Town. In the courtyard at Smith's Place, the brothers added laboratories, stables and a warehouse (now flats). The villa remains the company office and archive. Among the period features are Venetian windows, a New-Town-style fanlight and a cantilevered oval staircase. The 'greyhound' weathervane represents the Raimes's prize-winning racing dogs.

### E 14
**Cable Tramway Wheels**
Leith Walk at Iona Street

The city's Victorian tram network was replaced by buses in 1956. New trams began running from the airport to York Place in 2014. They came to Leith Walk in 2023 when the Trams to Newhaven project was completed.

The Victorian tramways serving Leith and Edinburgh were not connected. Edinburgh's trams were hauled by a steam-powered moving cable below the tracks (like the cable cars in San Francisco); Leith's were electric, powered from overhead wires.

During excavations for the Newhaven extension, two cable wheels (c. 1900) were found at the intersection of Pilrig Street and

Leith Walk. This was the boundary between Leith and Edinburgh until 1920 when the municipalities merged. Passengers had to change trams here until Edinburgh's trams were electrified in 1922. The inconvenience was called 'The Pilrig Muddle'. The historic cable wheels were restored and are displayed close to their original location.

E 15
**South Leith Parish Church Kirkyard**
Constitution Street and Kirkgate

The burial ground is filled with historic gravestones, carved and inscribed with skill and sensitivity by stonemasons unrecorded. Memento mori are plentiful: skulls, cherubs and angels, and trade symbols indicating the former occupations of the deceased.

In medieval times the kirkyard extended across what is now Constitution Street. Archeological digs in 2020 when the tramline to Newhaven was being constructed along the street revealed dozens of human skeletons, some dating from the 14th century.

E 16
**South Leith Parish Church**
Kirkgate

The 'Kirk of Leith' is more than five hundred years old (the first structure here was St Mary's chapel, recorded in 1483). The present building was once larger because in 1560 during the Siege of Leith the eastern section was destroyed by English artillery.

Architect Thomas Hamilton rebuilt the kirk in 1848 in Gothic Revival style. The 17th-century west tower, similar to the one in situ at St Ninian's Church, was replaced. The nave was reconstructed with a spectacular oak hammer beam roof. The stained glass windows are Victorian, from the Ballantine studio.

The tower and porch display the coats of arms of four successive

Scottish monarchs: Queen Regent Mary of Guise (widow of James V), her daughter Mary Queen of Scots, James VI and Charles I.

E 17
**Trinity House**
99 Kirkgate

A hospital and almshouse were founded here 1550s by the Fraternity of Shipmasters and Mariners of Leith, later incorporated as a trade guild to maintain lighthouses, collect port dues and help sailors and their families in need.

The coat of arms – with two globes, an anchor, compass and the fraternity's motto in Latin meaning 'Men of virtue can master the earth, the sea and the stars' – is set in the pediment at Trinity House. The villa (1818) was designed by Thomas Brown, architect of the Exchange Buildings.

Leith's maritime heritage is celebrated inside – a time capsule overflowing with ship models, paintings, maps and charts, books, navigational instruments and other memorabilia. Most impressive is

the Conveying Room upstairs. The ceiling and frieze are decorated with Adamesque plasterwork showing Neptune, ancient mariners, sailing ships, navigational tools, flying fish and dolphins. Dominating the room is a painting of 1842, *Vasco da Gama Encountering the Spirit of the Storm*.

E 18
**Exchange Buildings**
37–43 Constitution Street

The Exchange, funded by subscription, served the same purpose as the Royal Exchange in Edinburgh, namely a meeting place for merchants. It included a coffee house, reading rooms and offices behind a dignified classical façade in the manner of Robert Adam. The building (1810) incorporated the Assembly Hall of 1785, a venue for high society like the Assembly Rooms in Edinburgh.

E 19
**Robert Burns statue**
Constitution Street

The bronze statue was commissioned by Leith Burns Club and

erected in 1898. On each side of the sandstone plinth is a narrative panel inspired by the bard's work. The statue and plinth, removed in 2019 to make way for the Trams to Newhaven project, were reinstated in 2022.

Behind Burns is the domed Leith Corn Exchange, built in 1862 to a design by Peddie & Kinnear. The grain trade is symbolised on a Renaissance-style frieze by sculptor John Rhind on the Constitution Street façade.

E 20
**Lamb's House**
11 Waters Close

The building's pantiled steeply pitched roof, crow-stepped gables, harled walls and timber balcony have time-travelled from the 17th-century. Heavy timbers inside are original, thought to have been imported from Norway or Sweden. Pantiles came from trade with the Hanseatic League. Those on the recently renewed roof were sourced in Sweden.

The house was rented to the burgesses of Edinburgh who had exclusive mercantile rights to Leith Harbour. The ground floor was for trading. The merchant tenants occupied six flats accessed by a common stair. In the 1930s, the 4th Marquess of Bute saved the house from demolition; in 1958, his son gave it to the National Trust for Scotland. In 2010, it was bought by conservation architects Kristín Hannesdóttir and Nicholas Groves-Raines who restored and rehabilitated it as a live/work dwelling. The name recalls merchant Andro Lamb (see page 143).

E 21
**Ronaldson's Wharf**
Sandport Place

This attractive private and social

housing project was completed in 2005 on a previously derelict site. The 120 units are 'tenure-blind', meaning that the social housing, for Port of Leith Housing Association, looks as good as the private block, although the latter gets the views of the Water of Leith. Both types of tenure have wide eaves and timber and stucco surfaces, clearly contemporary – no fake heritage here.

This was not the first habitation on the site. Archaeological excavations uncovered traces of medieval occupation and later buildings, including Second World War air-raid shelters.

E 22
**St Ninian's Church and Manse**
Quayside Street

The narrative here goes back to 1493 when the Abbott of Holyrood established a chapel, rebuilt after the Reformation. In 1606, it became North Leith Parish Church with a manse said to be Leith's oldest building. The Dutch style belfry, a common type on Scotland's east coast, was built in 1675 (the date above the door).

The adjoining 18th-century tenement has an arched entrance that accessed the church. The keystone is a grotesque mask (maybe Father Time). Above it is an inscription: 'Blessed are they that hear the word of God and keep it.'

In 1816, the congregation moved to North Leith Parish Church. The old buildings here were absorbed,

and knocked about a bit, as part of McGregor & Company's Quayside Mills. Restoration around 2000 led by the Scottish Historic Buildings Trust with Simpson & Brown Architects recreated the 17th-century exteriors, with offices and flats inside. The correct limewash colour was reproduced and the tower and clock restored. The gilded copper weathercock is a copy of the original, now in the National Museum of Scotland.

E 23
**Leith Custom House**
65–67 Commercial Street

Leith was Scotland's premier port until eclipsed by Glasgow. Its status merited this Greek Revival customs house (1812) designed by architect Robert Reid. Royal authority was symbolised with lion and unicorn heraldry in the

portico's pediment above daunting Doric columns. Ship's captains, suitably impressed, would climb the forestair and venture inside to declare their cargoes and pay duties.

Vacated in 1980, the building was bought by the City in 2015. Since 2019 the Scottish Historic Buildings Trust has been working on its conservation and future use for the community.

E 24
**King's Wark**
36 The Shore, Leith Old Harbour

One of the oldest buildings in Leith is this early 18th-century tenement. The name recalls King's Wark (meaning 'work' in old Scots), a royal compound begun in 1434 by James I. The site included variously, and at various times, a royal residence, an armoury for the king's warships, workshops for shipwrights, a store-house for exports and imports, a wine cellar and even a tennis court; also facilities for merchants, a customs house and taverns. At one time, a plague hospital was here. Today, there is a bar/restaurant.

Nothing remains of the original complex which was largely destroyed by English troops during the invasion of 1544. The property was transferred to the magistrates of Edinburgh in 1647 and subsequently redeveloped. The tenement's traditional harling was applied during a 1970s restoration.

E 25
**35 The Shore**

A frenzy of Scots Baronial style with bartizans, cannon spouts, thistle and fleur-de-lis finials on

crowstepped gables, cast-iron gargoyles by the gutters and a spire for the two griffins on Bernard Street to fly around. Leith's motto is carved above the double doors. The building (1864), surely Leith's most eccentric, was built for local merchant, ship owner and politician Donald Robert MacGregor.

E 26
**The Ship on The Shore**
24–31 The Shore

The seafood restaurant so-called is on the ground floor of this tenement, once the Ship Inn, later the Old Ship Hotel. A plaque on the façade and a marker on the quayside opposite note the visit to Edinburgh by King George IV who disembarked on 'King's Landing' in 1822.

The model three-masted sailing ship at No. 28 is a replica of the Ship Inn's long-lost original sign. Above it is a stone-carved galleon in full sail, dated 1676, thought to have been salvaged when the tenement was reconstructed in the 1880s.

E 27
**Malmaison Hotel**
1 Tower Place

No other building represents better Leith's shift from maritime tradition to trendiness. The Malmaison opened in 1994 as the district's first boutique hotel. It occupies the Scots Baronial-style former Leith Sailors' Home built in the 1880s to accommodate ships' officers and sailors, and those rescued from shipwrecks.

On Tower Place is the Merchant Navy Memorial, a sandstone column erected in 2010 in memory of Scottish mariners lost at sea. Bronze reliefs and an interpretive panel recall the ships on which they served and the hazards they faced. Nearby is the drum-shaped Signal Tower built in 1686 as a windmill. From battlements added during the Napoleonic Wars flags were flown to communicate tidal conditions to ships waiting to enter the harbour.

### E 28
**The Whalers' Memorial**

On the edge of Tower Place is a harpoon gun from a ship owned by Leith-based Christian Salvesen. The company's Antarctic whaling fleet was once the world's largest. Leith mariners had hunted whales in the Arctic from the 1600s until the mid 19th century when the resource was depleted and whaling shifted to the south Atlantic.

### E 29
**Victoria Swing Bridge**

Re-painted and re-decked by Forth Ports in 2024, this 1870s wrought-iron, bowstring trussed bridge crossing the Water of Leith used to swing open for ships to enter and leave the Old Harbour. Its

hydraulically powered and counterweighted cantilevered span was the longest of its type in Britain. Railway tracks served Commercial Quay and Victoria Dock. No trains now: only pedestrians and cyclists.

### E 30
**Prince of Wales Dry Dock Pumping Station**
*Alexander Rendel engineer 1860*

The lock gates once here were activated by hydraulic power from steam-driven pumps in the pumping station. You wouldn't know this from how the building and its water tower appear – Victorian industrial architecture dressed up in a historical style, here Italianate.

### E 31
**Port of Leith Distillery**
11 Whisky Quay
*Threesixty Architecture 2023*

Whisky is not new to Leith where the 'water of life' has been traditionally stored in bonded warehouses for maturation, sale and export. This new distillery is something else. Built on a site constrained by water on two sides, the steel-framed nine storey

structure is Scotland's first vertical distillery. It towers above Leith docks, the Royal Yacht *Britannia* and Ocean Terminal mall.

Inside, there is an energy saving gravitational process – grain milling and mashing at the top, descending through fermentation to the hand-crafted copper stills. The barley used is locally sourced and malted, cutting food miles and the carbon footprint. Branding includes the name painted on the tower. The visitor centre has spectacular views.

### E 32
### Victoria Quay

Constructed on derelict docklands, this 1990s office block was inherited from the British Government's Scottish Office when the Scotland Act 1998 created a Scottish gov-

ernment. Designed to house 1,500 civil servants, the building, 250 metres long with a superstructure like the deck and funnel of a great ship, launched Leith's regeneration

Nearby is Commercial Quay with a row of 19th-century bonded warehouses repurposed with offices, co-working spaces, an artisan café and Michelin-star dining – the new Leith reinvigorating the old.

# Tour F
# Beyond the city centre

*Duddingston Kirk*

*Thomson's Tower*

*Portobello Swim Centre*

*St John the Evangelist Church*

*Robin Chapel*

*Craigmillar Castle*

*Bridgend Farm*

*Rosslyn Chapel*

*Water of Leith Visitor Centre*

*Saughton Park*

*Colinton Parish Church*

*Colinton Tunnel*

*Jupiter Artland*

*The Wealth of Nations sculpture*

*Craigsbank Church*

*Lauriston Castle*

*Granton Castle Walled Garden*

*Cramond Harbour*

*Dalmeny Kirk*

*The Forth Railway Bridge*

Opposite: *Corstorphine Old Parish Church. Corstorphine is one of several villages around Edinburgh consumed by suburban development in the late 19th and early 20th centuries. It became officially part of Edinburgh in 1920. Traces of the past remain. The stone spire of the 15th-century parish church was a landmark in the surrounding farmland from where dairy produce, fruit and vegetables were sent to market in the city.*

# EDINBURGH'S BEST BUILDINGS

Tour F—**BEYOND THE CITY CENTRE**

## F 1
**Duddingston Kirk**
Old Church Lane

Duddingston Village hugs the shore of Duddingston Loch, a wildlife reserve since 1923. The setting below Arthur's Seat could be the Highlands but it's only three kilometres from Princes Street.

History is embedded in the 12th-century kirk's stones, the oldest being those on the Romanesque doorway (the original entrance) on the south wall. The north wall was rebuilt in 1631 to accommodate an internal gallery known as the Prestonfield Aisle, funded by and for a typically privileged local laird.

The kirk was restored by Robert Rowand Anderson in 1889. The entrance today, an oak door on the north wall, was installed in 1922 as a First War memorial along with a commemorative tablet. On the south wall, beside the Gothic window to the chancel, there is a finely carved baroque memento mori dated 1693.

The 19th-century gatehouse like a miniature castle was a watch tower built to protect the kirk's burial ground from Edinburgh's body-snatchers.

## F 2
**Thomson's Tower**
Dr Neil's Garden, Old Church Lane

William Playfair designed this octagonal curiosity in 1825 for the Duddingston Curling Society whose curling stones were stored on the ground floor. Upstairs was an art studio for landscape painter the Rev. John Thomson, minister from 1805 to 1840 at Duddingston

Kirk. J M W Turner, when observing Duddingston Loch, is said to have remarked, 'By God sir, I envy you that piece of water'. Another artist Thomson knew was Henry Raeburn who chose the loch as the setting for *The Skating Minister*, displayed in the National Gallery.

The tower stands in 'Edinburgh's secret garden' created in 1963 by two doctors, Nancy and Andrew Neil. The enchanted landscape and the tower have been maintained by Dr Neil's Garden Trust since 1997.

F 3
**Craigentinny Marbles**
Craigentinny Crescent

A Roman-style mausoleum lost in a suburb of 1920s bungalows. The 'marbles' illustrate biblical scenes. The deceased was William Henry Mille of Craigentinny estate, a politician, antiquarian and eccentric. In 1848, he was buried in a stone-lined vault he specified to be 12 metres below where his monumental gravestone was erected a decade later.

F 4
**Schultz Chocolate Factory**
102 Inchview Terrace

Messrs. Schultz Continental Chocolate Factory was established by German-born merchant Charles William Schultz and run by his three sons. The reinforced concrete structure (1906), advanced for its time, is concealed by a brick coating in Edwardian classical style.

German workers, most of them women, were employed until the First World War when the building was requisitioned for a barracks. Schultz was declared an 'enemy alien'. Two of his sons were killed serving with the British army in France. After the war, the factory became the W M Ramsay Technical Institute. The building was filled with flats in 1995.

### F 5
**The Tower**
Figgate Lane, Portobello

Portobello has a rich and varied built heritage often surprising, like this Gothic folly built in 1785 as a summer house for John Cunningham, a lawyer. The octagonal tower incorporates stones from medieval times to the 17th century salvaged from Edinburgh's Old Town. A door lintel dated 1674 has an inscription in Latin: *Pax Intrantibvs Salvs Exevntibvs* meaning 'Peace to those who enter, health to those who leave.'

### F 6
**The Kilns**
Bridge Street

The bottle kilns were built for the A W Buchan & Co. Thistle Pottery, one of several in Portobello where clay suitable for stoneware storage jars had been discovered in the 18th century. The pottery closed in 1972 after 200 years here. Portobello Heritage Trust campaigned to save the kilns which were the only ones surviving in Scotland. The 1909 kiln was rebuilt in 2013 (the year is marked on a new brick). Its twin of 1906 in danger of collapse was dismantled in 2019. The base was protected pending restoration.

### F 7
**Portobello Swim Centre**
The Promenade
*Robert Morham, City Architect*

Opened in 1901 as Portobello Sea Water Baths this flagship amenity was proclaimed 'the most modern in Britain', with men's and women's heated pools and Turkish baths. All are well preserved and popular having been recently restored. The façade displays carved coats of arms of Portobello and Edinburgh marking the municipalities' amalgamation at the time.

### F 8
### Portobello and Joppa Parish Church
1 Brunstane Road North

Built as Portobello Free Church (1877) by Glasgow architect John Honeyman. The firm Honeyman, Keppie & Mackintosh fitted a new church organ in 1906, for which Charles Rennie Mackintosh designed a Gothic timber screen.

The organ was removed in the 1960s along with the screen (its fate unknown). It is unlikely they would have survived the fire that destroyed the timber roof and gutted the interior in 1998. Firefighters saved the stone structure, tower and steeple. Reconstruction kept the arcades and aisles in the nave. The outstanding feature is two stained and painted glass windows that replaced those fatally damaged by the fire.

### F 9
### Portobello Old Parish Church
16b Bellfield Street
*William Sibbald 1809*

A Georgian gem with an elegantly carved date stone above the fanlight in the doorway and Gothic tracery in the upper windows. The clock tower (1839) has Roman Doric pilasters, an octagonal belfry, cupola and weathercock.

When the congregation moved to Portobello & Joppa Parish Church in 2014 the old property was threatened with residential redevelopment. This was prevented thanks to activism that invoked the Scottish Government's community 'right to buy' legislation, the first time it was used in an urban context.

The church, and its modernist hall by architects Alan Reiach & Partners (1964), were renamed 'Bellfield' and reopened as a community centre in 2018.

F 10
**Japanese House**
11a Bellfield Lane
*Konishi Gaffney Architects 2009*

Portobello's lanes are a collage of cottages, garages, old workshops and stables. The best new buildings, like this self-build, by and for the architects, fit the urban grain and serendipity. Seen from the lane the energy-efficient, timber-framed house is Scottish vernacular with oak cladding. The Japanese aspect, concealed from passersby, is a seamless transition from a minimalist open-plan living space to the walled garden.

F 11
**26BS (26 Bath Street)**
*John Kinsley Architects 2017*

This self-build project was planned and procured by the families that live here. It reinterprets the traditional Scottish tenement, an example of which is next door. The façade fits the height of the tenement and steps down with courtesy to the other neighbour, a 19th-century terrace. The sandstone cladding is considerate of local heritage character. The structure is contemporary, consisting of cross-laminated timber manufactured off-site. It was erected in nine days by three joiners. Renewable energy is sourced and insulation is to Passivhaus standards.

F 12
**Portobello Police Station**
118 High Street

Portobello, a separate burgh from Edinburgh until in 1896, had its own town halls. One of them, dated 1863, can be seen at 189 High Street. It was built on the site of an 18th-century cottage said to

have been called 'Puerto Bello' by a resident who had been at the capture of Puerto Bello, Panama by the Royal Navy in 1739, hence the burgh's name.

The Police Scotland station was a later town hall and public library, opened in 1877. No confusion about its style – the crow-stepped gables, bartizans and a French tower with a cast-iron crown are typical Scots Baronial features. The library was relocated in 1963 and the police occupied the whole building. Another local hall (1914), in Edwardian classical style at 147–149 High Street, is now a community-run venue.

F 13
**St John the Evangelist Catholic Church**
35 Brighton Place

Soaring out of the 19th-century neighbourhood that is Brighton Park are the neo-Gothic pinnacles of St John's Church (1906) like nothing else in Edinburgh.

The nave is a powerful space. Pillars with carved angels holding scrolls support the arches on arcaded aisles. Light is beamed in from Gothic clerestories. The timber roof is a boat-shaped barrel vault. The chancel glows with stained glass windows illustrating the Nativity, Crucifixion and Resurrection. The Last Supper is painted on the altar.

Architect James Thomas Walford, a member of the church previously resident in London, is

said to have waived his fee, blessed with this late-career achievement.

F 14
**Robin Chapel**
Thistle Foundation, Queen's Walk
*John Fraser Matthew 1950–53*

This poignant memorial chapel was commissioned by the parents of Lieutenant Robin Tudsbery of the Royal Horse Guards who was killed in action a few days before the end of the Second World War.

Every part of the chapel is beautifully crafted in a late flowering of Arts and Crafts style. The medieval-style belfry is partly crow-stepped; the sanctuary is roofed with ancient Ballachulish slate; stones were quarried in Northumberland. The west front is rusticated, with masonry surrounding the stained glass cross

patterned like a halo. A symbolic robin is perched on the wrought-iron finial.

A barrel-vaulted ceiling runs the length of the nave. East Lothian oak pews and the pulpit feature carved animals and birds. Robin Tudsbery was a nature-lover, but in the glorious east window by artist Sadie McLellan he is cavalry officer, stylised in stained glass as a charioteer entering Heaven. Nine other windows by McLellan represent scenes from *The Pilgrim's Progress*.

F 15
**Thistle Foundation Centre of Wellbeing**
Queen's Walk

The community centre (3DReid Architects 2016) is located in a village of row houses built in 1950 by the Thistle Foundation to help disabled ex-service personnel live independently. The charity, established in 1944 by Sir Francis and Lady Tudsbery, continues to support people living with long-term health issues.

Spaces around the centre's bright and welcoming reception hub are naturally lit and flexible. Eco-friendly timber is deployed inside and out. The name formed in the timber cladding reflects the depth of the cross in the stonework at the Thistle Foundation's Robin Chapel nearby.

F 16
**Craigmillar Castle**
Craigmillar Castle Road

'Edinburgh's other castle', a ruin since the 18th century, is layered with 16th- and 17th-century accretions around a 14th-century tower house. An outer courtyard was added in the 15th century, protected by massive walls and flanking towers.

The castle was built by the Prestons of Craigmillar, whose property it was from 1374 to 1660. Family life was focused around the huge hearth in the vaulted Great Hall, a lofty space surrounded by a vertical maze of ancillary rooms and spiral stairs. Footsteps and voices of visitors today are mysteriously amplified, or are they ghosts?

In 1544, when Henry VIII ordered the Earl of Hereford to 'put all to fire and sword, burn Edinburgh town', Craigmillar Castle was surrendered without a fight to the English invaders, who burned it anyway.

Association with Mary Queen of Scots adds frisson to its empty spaces. Here in 1566, the Earl of Bothwell and fellow conspirators are said to have planned the murder of Mary's second husband, Lord Darnley. After the deed was done – gunpowder bomb in Kirk o' Field House (later the site of the Old College) and Darnley and his servant strangled as they fled – she married Bothwell. Her presence with a retinue of French courtiers gave the castle and the local district the name Little France.

F 17
**Bridgend Farm**
41 Old Dalkeith Road

An 18th-century farmhouse on land that was part of Craigmillar Castle estate. The City could have sold the derelict property for commercial development. Instead, community ownership was agreed in 2015 following a plan to restore the house and former farm as a model of sustainability.

The site has been transformed by volunteers, with architects Malcolm Fraser and Halliday Fraser Munro, as an activity and learning centre. The farmhouse has a café, training kitchen and meeting rooms. There are outdoor play areas, a theatrical stage and allotments. The row of community workshops, timber-framed with charred larch cladding, was built in 2018. Also timber-framed is the recent straw bale-insulated Eco Bothy built in partnership with the Scottish Ecological Design Association. Inside, a cut-out exposes a piece of straw bale.

F 18
**Craigend Park**
84 Kingston Avenue
*Frederick Thomas Pilkington 1869*

Pilkington was a wizard of creepy Victorian Gothic. By day, his buildings are simply strange, at

night, sinister. Craigend has all the trimmings: spiky tower, carved cornucopia, chimera on a drainpipe, Green Man above the loggia, and a ghostly hall with a baronial staircase.

The owner was a tailor with a shop on prestigious George Street. From 1918 to 1925, Craigend was a hospital for shell-shocked soldiers, later Kingston Clinic for alternative medical therapy. It was subdivided in the 1980s for flats.

F 19
**Liberton Kirk**
Kirkgate

An early Gothic Revival church (1815) built in what was a rural setting, now a suburban (Liberton became a part of the City of Edinburgh in 1920).

Picturesque with pinnacles, crenellated parapets and a coat of ivy, the kirk designed by James Gillespie Graham was funded by the 'heritors', the feudal landowners of the parish. It replaced a fire-damaged earlier building. The parish dates from the 12th century but is thought to have been a Christian site long before then. An ancient Celtic cross found here inspired the kirk's emblem.

F 20
**Mortonhall Crematorium**
30b Howden Hall Road
*Basil Spence, Glover & Ferguson 1967*

The real world recedes on the long path through woodland to a clearing where this secular starship waits to spirit the dead away. The crematorium's chapel is an austere yet soothing nave-like space with a central aisle along which coffin bearers carry their load. The space narrows to focus

on a top-lit void, expressed outside as spire. Walls are vertical slabs with narrow strips of stained glass casting coloured light on the chapel's white plaster walls. Spence achieved timelessness here: the building will never grow old.

F 21
**Rosslyn Chapel**
Chapel Loan, Roslin Village

It took 40 years for skilled workers, many 'from other regions and foreign kingdoms', to construct and decorate Rosslyn Chapel, begun in 1446 by William St Clair for his family. Excavations in the 19th century revealed foundations thought to indicate a cruciform plan. These would have made the chapel twice the size, but William died in 1484 and with him the more ambitious design.

Protestant zealots during the Reformation denounced it a 'house and monument of idolatrie' and in 1592 ordered the altars destroyed. Oliver Cromwell stabled horses in the chapel in 1650 when his troops attacked nearby Rosslyn Castle.

In 1862, the chapel was restored by architect David Bryce for the 3rd Earl of Rosslyn and rededicated by the Episcopal Bishop of Edinburgh. Rosslyn Chapel Trust was formed in 1995 to conserve the building and protect its pastoral setting.

The exterior bristles with flying buttresses, Gothic tracery and pinnacles. Inside, there is a deluge of decoration. Almost every surface is covered with medieval stone carvings of exceptional

quality, especially on the ceiling in the nave and on the Apprentice Pillar, said to be haunted by the boy who carved it.

The chapel became an iconic attraction after being featured in the 2003 novel and subsequent film *The Da Vinci Code*, which popularised long-held speculation that the site is linked to the Knights Templar and the Holy Grail.

Rosslyn gained record numbers of sightseers and funds for conservation and a Visitor Centre, sensitively designed by Page\Park Architects, which opened in 2011.

F 22
**Fairmilehead Parish Church**
1a Frogston Road West
*Leslie Grahame Thomson 1938*

Ogee-roofed and gabled, the tower looks more Scandinavian than Scottish. The plan is conventional with a nave, transepts and apse, but column-free with a striking white-rendered parabolic ceiling. The minimalist interior was avant-garde for Edinburgh of the time and is still a surprise.

F 23
**Craiglockhart Hospital**
Edinburgh Napier University
219 Colinton Road
*Peddie & Kinnear 1877–80*

Opened as a hydropathic hospital, the Italianate building was used by the military during the First World War for officers needing treatment for psychological stress and shell shock. Among them were the soldier poets Siegfried Sassoon and Wilfred Owen. Sassoon recalled the place 'sepulchral and oppressive, redeemed only by its healthy situation and pleasant view of the Pentland Hills.'

Subsequently, the building was the Convent of the Sacred Heart and a teacher training college. It is now Napier University's Business School. Displayed inside is the university's War Poets Collection.

F 24
**Water of Leith Visitor Centre**
24 Lanark Road
*Malcolm Fraser Architects 2000*

The Water of Leith flows for 35 kilometres from its source in the Pentland Hills to the sea at Leith. Dozens of mills once processed

cloth, paper, lumber, flour and snuff, and polluted the water. The environment has since recovered. History and the natural habitat are explained in the centre, run by the Water of Leith Conservation Trust.

The building is a renovated but externally unaltered Victorian school house, to which was added a timber extension astride the Water of Leith Walkway.

F 25
**Saughton Park**
Balgreen Road

A 17th-century country estate bought by the City in 1900, the park was famously the site of the 1908 Scottish National Exhibition of agriculture, engineering and horticulture. Exhibition Bridge still spans the Water of Leith at Gorgie Road, but the glory days faded and the park decayed.

It was restored in 2019 by the City, the Royal Caledonian Horticultural Society, Friends of Saughton Park and Sutherland Hussey Harris Architects. The Royal Promenade of 1908 and the former estate's Walled Garden were spruced up. The Stable Block became a community venue, café and base for the RCHS.

The Edwardian cast-iron Lion Foundry bandstand, removed in the 1980s and stored in pieces off-site, was recovered, restored and reassembled. Micro-hydro technology on the Water of Leith generates electricity, making Saughton the first fully eco-powered green space in Britain.

F 26
**St Cuthbert's Episcopal Church**
6 Westgarth Avenue
*Robert Rowand Anderson 1888–94*

R R Anderson was a founding member of this Arts and Crafts church, distinguished by its belfry, designed in 17th-century Dutch

style, and richly endowed interior. The timber ceiling with stencilled decoration was inspired by 16th-century examples in the Old Town. The stained glass widows, especially the West (or 'founders window') are especially fine.

The church was built when Colinton village grew as a commuter suburb with the arrival of the Caledonian railway. Anderson, who helped fund the construction of the church, lived at 'Allermuir' (1879), a Scots Baronial villa he designed at 15 Woodhall Road.

F 27
**Colinton Parish Church**
Dell Road

The church is known for its association with Robert Louis Stevenson whose grandfather, Lewis Balfour, was the minister. Stevenson's *A Child's Garden of Verses* was inspired in part from visits the writer made here as a boy. The statue of him, with two books and his Skye terrier, was installed by Colinton Community Conservation Trust, and there is a poetry trail, 'A Walk with Robert Louis Stevenson'.

An inscription on the kirk's west side notes '1771', the year when the church of 1650 was rebuilt. A board in the vestibule tells that the parish dates from around 1095.

The church RLS knew was reconstructed in 1908 by architect Sydney Mitchell, incorporating the Italianate tower of 1837 designed by David Bryce. Angels hover in the nave; the neo-Byzantine half-domed apse is decorated with Art Nouveau stencilled vine patterns.

Among the kirkyard's row of mausoleums are the Balfour family tomb and that of James Gillespie of Spylaw House.

F 28
**Spylaw House**
Spylaw Park, 25 Spylaw Street

Hidden in a glen of the Water of Leith is this handsome house with a Georgian frontage, added in 1773. At the back are the remains

of the 17th-century Spylaw Mill.

The property, now a public park, belonged to James Gillespie who made a fortune as a tobacco dealer and snuff manufacturer. With his brother John, he ran a tobacco shop on the Royal Mile. In 1797, he bequeathed to the Merchant Company his Colinton estate and money to build and endow a hospital for the elderly and a free school for poor boys, now James Gillespie's High School.

F 29
**Colinton Tunnel**
Water of Leith Walkway

'Scotland's longest heritage mural', painted in 2020 by artist Chris Rutterford and a team of muralists, school children and other volunteers, decorates this tunnel constructed in 1874 by the Caledonian Railway on its line from Princes Street Station to Balerno.

Local history is the theme, inspired by Robert Louis Stevenson's poem *From a Railway Carriage*. His verse is featured; so is he, at his writing desk and looking out from a railway carriage.

F 30
**William Fraser Homes**
52 Spylaw Bank Road
*A F Balfour Paul 1899*

Sited on the plateau above the Water of Leith, this charming ensemble is set around a landscaped courtyard framed by pavilions. The dwellings were built as alms houses 'to house poor persons of good character over the age of 55, with preference given to authors and artists.' They were endowed by archivist, historian and University of Edinburgh professor Sir William Fraser and run by a board of trustees.

The architecture is Scottish vernacular in 17th-century style, no doubt influenced by Robert Rowand Anderson with whom Balfour Paul had trained.

F 31
**Jupiter Artland**
Bonnington House Steadings
Wilkieston

In 2009, the owners of Bonnington House opened Jupiter Artland – art *en plein air* for everyone. From the 'Sputnik' entrance gates to the

historic steading, contemporary artworks pop up everywhere.

This cosmic fusion of art and landscape features *Cells of Life* (an earthwork similar to that at the Gallery of Modern Art), created by Charles Jencks; *Rose Walk* by Pablo Bronstein – a lattice-fenced pathway with a gazebo at each end, one chinoiserie, the other Gothic – a play on the fashion since the Renaissance for eccentric and exotic garden follies; and *Love Bomb* (Marc Quinn), a 12-metre high orchid, surreal like the 19th-century curiosities on Calton Hill. There are many more installations by national and international artists, some hidden in woodland, others in plain sight, and new works appear as if by magic.

The steading was repurposed for temporary exhibitions and as a café/restaurant by Benjamin Tindall Architects who also drew up the masterplan that guided the landscape design.

F 32
**Air Traffic Control Tower**
Edinburgh Airport
*3DReid Architects, Arup engineers*
*2005*

Form follows function, clad with diamond-shaped aluminium panels that conceal a concrete service core in this sculptural control tower.

At the top is a floor slab on which the control room is perched. The tower, 57 metres high, gives controllers a 360° view. At night LED luminaries colour the structure which inspired a new logo for the airport.

Originally a First World War airfield, the airport was later RAF Turnhouse, home of 603 (City of Edinburgh) Squadron. A Second World War memorial (a replica Spitfire) is across from the Control Tower on the approach road to the terminal where commercial flights started in 1947.

F 33
**'The Wealth of Nations'**
Royal Bank of Scotland Headquarters, 175 Glasgow Road Gogarburn

This giant sculpture by Eduardo Paolozzi was commissioned by RBS. First installed as part of the public art programme at Edinburgh Park (the business park promoted by the City in the 1990s), it was relocated to Gogarburn in 2021. Adam Smith's book inspired the title. Hands on the levers of power suggest not a banker but a creator. The sculpture's base has a quote from Albert Einstein: 'Knowledge is wonderful, but imagination is even better.'

F 34
**Craigsbank Church**
19 Craigs Bank

The kirk was founded by the Church of Scotland in 1937. In the 1960s, the congregation outgrew its traditional stone building (now the church hall). Architects Rowand Anderson, Kininmonth & Paul were hired to provide more space. They did so with this striking modernist box, its concave bell tower like a sail on the community's sea of 1920s bungalows.

The square-plan interior has seating tiered on three sides; pulpit, crucifix and the organ are on the fourth side. Natural light is distributed indirectly from the fringes of a 'floating' ceiling. The sunken sanctuary is said to symbolise the hidden hillside hollows where Covenanters worshipped during the 'killing times' of the 17th century.

F 35
**Corstorphine Doocot**
Dovecot Road

This 16th-century beehive-shaped doocot was associated with Corstorphine Castle on the Forrester

family estate. The castle was torn down in the 19th century. The doocot with 1,060 nesting boxes in 28 rows supplied pigeon meat and eggs for the castle table and guano to fertilise the gardens. Cottages here once housed tapestry workshops, since relocated and now Dovecot Studios.

F 36
**Corstorphine Old Parish Church**
Kirk Loan

The architecture of this parish church is the result of additions and alterations made since the 15th century. The roof is stone-slabbed and the square-plan tower sprouts an octagonal stone spire. The north transept of 1646 was enlarged by William Burn in 1828; the vaulted nave was reconstructed in 1905. The west porch is said to contain stones from the 12th-century St. Mary's church which was nearby until demolished during the Reformation. The tower houses a bell cast in 1728.

The church can be traced back to a family chapel built by the laird of Corstorphine, merchant Adam Forrester, Lord Provost of Edinburgh. The carved effigy of a knight in armour in the nave represents one of the Forresters with his faithful dog.

Outside, in a niche above the east window, a lamp symbolises a tradition since medieval times, when the light at night guided travellers, and Corstorphine's villagers home. Corstorphine Heritage Centre nearby, in one of Edinburgh's oldest inhabited buildings, tells the story of the village and its people.

F 37
**St Anne's Parish Church**
1 Kames Road at St John's Road
*Peter Macgregor Chalmers 1913*

Beautifully crafted and almost complete, this Romanesque Revival church only lacks the campanile planned for the entrance but not built due to the First World War.

The porch, with figures of Christ, the Four Evangelists, angels and the signs of the zodiac, leads to an arcaded nave with clerestory windows and apse. The Reverend John A Robertson, the first minister, desired that 'the stones speak' – the capitals on

the columns lining the aisles are carved with biblical themes.

In the apse there are three stained glass windows installed in 1917, created by Alf Webster. Sadly, he never saw them in situ having been killed on active service in France in 1915. The two flanking windows (1953) were by his son Gordon, who designed most of the other windows in the church. The pair in the vestibule, by William Wilson (1948), honour minister John Robertson. The architecture matches his motto: 'Only the best for St Anne's'.

F 38
**Falcon Hall Gates**
Edinburgh Zoo
134 Corstorphine Road

The Zoological Society of Scotland was established in 1909 by lawyer and natural history enthusiast Thomas Gillespie. The society, supported by the City, bought Corstorphine Hill House estate and developed it as the Scottish Zoological Park, now Edinburgh Zoo, which opened in 1913.

The cast-iron gates, decorative urns and two stone eagles were part of the original entrance. They were relocated here from Falcon Hall, a mansion in Morningside demolished in 1909 (its portico was reconstructed and can be seen at Bartholomew House).

F 39
**Caroline Park House**
Caroline Park Avenue, Granton

Hidden by trees, this country house dating from the 16th century was owned by a succession of aristocrats who made significant additions. The French style front facing the garden was built in 1696. The 2nd Duke of Argyll, who bought the property and Granton Castle in 1739, named it after his daughter Caroline, Countess of Dalkeith.

Later owned by the Dukes of

Buccleuch, Caroline Park House was leased in the 19th century as offices for A B Fleming and Co. whose printing ink factory was nearby. In the 1980s, the house was sold and returned to domestic use.

The entrance is on Caroline Park Avenue. The house can also be glimpsed from Waterfront Avenue where symbolic gate posts have been erected, replicating those now isolated above West Shore Road.

F 40
**1 Waterfront Avenue**
*Foster + Partners 2003*

The first project in Edinburgh by global architects Foster + Partners was this energy-efficient box wrapped with aluminium solar shades. Opened as Scottish Gas Headquarters, the building launched the architects' Granton Waterfront masterplan. The plan, commissioned by the City to transform Granton from post-industrial decay to a sustainable community, continues to evolve.

Directly west is ForthQuarter Park, a biodiverse habitat for wildlife and people. An environmental clean-up was required before the masterplan could implemented.

F 41
**Granton Gasworks Station**
Waterfront Broadway

Granton Gasworks, built in 1903 by the Edinburgh and Leith Corporation Gas Commissioners, was so large that it had its own railway station, designed by the Commissioners' engineer, W R Herring. It closed in 1942. The long-neglected building was acquired by the City in 2018 and was reopened in 2023, refurbished by ADP Architecture as a social and creative enterprises hub operated by Wasps Studios.

Nearby is the steel frame of the sole surviving gas holder (1901), repurposed to enclose a public park and events space.

F 42
**Madelvic House**
33 Granton Park Avenue

This was the office of the Madelvic Motor Carriage Company, founded in 1899 by City Astronomer William Peck to exploit electric technology. The company made battery-powered vehicles driven by a fifth wheel, which inspired the logo above the door. They were

tested as taxis but not a success. Madelvic, ahead of its time, went bankrupt in 1900.

### F 43
**Social Bite Village**
West Shore Road

Social Bite, a startup to help feed and employ street people, opened a sandwich shop on Edinburgh's Rose Street in 2012. In 2018, the social enterprise opened this temporary village for homeless folk on land leased from the City.

The village, managed by charity parter Cyrenians, has provided a safe haven and practical help for 100 people experiencing homelessness. Its ten 'NestHouses' – modular and eco-friendly with sustainable timber – were designed for relocation, because the site is part of the Granton Waterfront development plans. The lease expired in 2024. A new site has been found, further along West Shore Road.

### F 44
**Granton Castle Walled Garden**
Speirs Bruce Way

The 16th-century Granton Castle estate included this walled garden, the oldest to survive in Edinburgh. In 1921, the castle, by then a ruin undermined by quarrying, was demolished. The Ministry of Works had tried to save it but sent a preservation order to the wrong address. All that remains are the boundary wall and doocot.

The garden has been owned by the City since 2005. It was overgrown until the Friends of the Walled Garden gained access in 2017 to restore it as an accessible biodiverse resource, following a campaign to save it from redevelopment as luxury housing.

### F 45
**Lauriston Castle**
Cramond Road South

A 16th-century tower house with additions made in the 19th century, and Edwardian interiors

created after William Reid, owner of cabinet makers Morison & Company, bought it in 1902.

The tower house was built by the Napiers of Merchiston on lands once held by the Forresters of Corstorphine. It was extended by William Burn in 1827 and, around 1845, by William Playfair who added the gabled porches and landscaped the grounds. There are monkey puzzle trees, an Italian garden, croquet lawn and a recent Japanese garden.

The Reid family gifted the seaview property to the City in 1926. The castle is preserved as they left it, furnished with impeccable taste showing the lifestyle they enjoyed.

F 46
**Cramond Kirk**
Cramond Glebe Road

The parish has been a Christian site since the 6th century. The land, where the River Almond enters the Forth, was once a Roman fort (its footprint, marked by archaeologists, can be seen in the park behind the kirk).

The medieval kirk was rebuilt in 1656 (the tower and a slab-roofed stone vault at the east gable are relics of it). The tower houses a 17th-century Dutch bell which was stolen for its valuable metal by Cromwell's troops in 1651. An appeal to their commander, General Monk, got it back. The hammer beam roof was fitted in 1911.

At the gate is the former counting house (since 2014, the Little Gatehouse Gallery) where Sunday collections were kept in a wall safe. The nearby manse was home to Robert Walker, immortalised in Henry Raeburn's painting *The Skating Minister*.

F 47
**Cramond Harbour**
Cramond's charm conceals an industrial heritage of grain mills

and iron works on the banks of the River Almond. By the mid 19th century only traces of those industries were left. The three-storey tenement on the quayside once housed workers and their families in 36 tiny flats, each with its own fireplace and chimney (hence the massed stacks visible today). The community's history is told by Cramond Heritage Trust in The Maltings, a former brewhouse and inn on the quayside.

On the tidal flats is a line of concrete posts. It's tempting to imagine them as Roman, but they were part of anti-submarine defences to protect the Royal Navy base at Rosyth during the Second World War.

## F 48
**Dalmeny Kirk**
Main Street, Dalmeny

Established in the 12th century, this is most complete Romanesque parish church in Scotland. The south doorway displays a weathered but largely intact bestiary and signs of the zodiac. Arches to the vaulted chancel and apse are patterned with chevrons typical of Romanesque style. Ceiling ribs spring from corbels carved as human and animal heads.

Construction of the Rosebery Aisle, a private space for the Earl of Rosebery and his family to worship, enlarged the kirk in 1671. The medieval bell tower is long gone (there is no record when), but restoration work (1927–37)

planned by architect Peter Macgregor Chalmers saw a new tower constructed to fit the historic fabric. The kirkyard is planted with gravestones from the 17th century. A stone coffin remains hollowed out to perfectly fit a corpse.

Not far from here is Kirkliston Parish Church, also 12th-century Romanesque.

## F 49
**Priory Church of St Mary of Mount Carmel**
Hopeton Road, South Queensferry

This 15th-century church is South Queensferry's oldest building. It evolved from a Carmelite friary built around 1330 on land granted

by the Dundas family. The Priory was Queensferry Parish Church until 1633 when a new one was built off the High Street. The old building was later used as a school, a net loft and stables. By the 1870s, it was roofless. It was restored in 1890 and reconsecrated for the Scottish Episcopal Church. Dundas memorials decorate the chancel.

F 50
**Black Castle**
38–40 High Street

The street is lined with buildings dating from the 17th century, none more daunting than the 'Castle', harled and dour in a coat of black paint. Built in 1626, it is South Queensferry's oldest house. Clues to its past are initials, hearts and love knots on the dormer window pediments. The letters 'WL' refer to merchant William Lowrie whose family was caught up in the witch hunts of the 17th century.

It has been said that there was a secret stair inside and a tunnel to the beach for smugglers landing contraband, but no such stair or tunnel have been found. The colour and harling were applied over the original stonework in the 1960s.

Steps beside Black Castle lead to the Parish Church of 1633 and the Vennel Kirkyard. Gravestones here date from the 17th century. Some are carved with navigational instruments and anchors (one with a three-masted vessel in full sail), recalling ship's captains, sailors of the Royal Navy, and local merchants who traded across the North Sea to Scandinavia and the Baltic ports.

F 51
**The Hawes Inn**
South Queensferry

South and North Queensferry are named after a ferry service begun in the 11th century by Queen Margaret for free passage of pilgrims to the holy sites at Dunfermline and St Andrews. The ferry also shortened the journey between the royal palace at Dunfermline and Edinburgh Castle. The first landing place was near Priory Church.

The Reformation stopped the

pilgrims but the ferry service continued. A new slipway was built in 1812 directly outside the Hawes Inn. When the Forth Road Bridge opened in 1964, the ferry, by that time a car ferry, was discontinued.

The inn dates from the 17th century. Robert Louis Stevenson is said to have written part of *Kidnapped* while lodging here in 1886. South Queensferry is a key location in the novel.

F 52
**The Forth Railway Bridge**
South Queensferry

The Forth estuary is unique, having three bridges side by side spanning three centuries: Queensferry Crossing (2017), the Forth Road Bridge (1964) and the Forth Railway Bridge (1890). Each represents the engineering expertise of its era: cable-stayed, suspension and cantilever.

The most famous is the Forth Railway Bridge. This supreme example of Victorian engineering replaced the Granton train ferry during a period of intense competition between railway companies to provide the fastest route from London to northeast Scotland. Two wide and windy river estuaries had to be crossed: the Forth and the Tay.

The 2.5-kilometre long railway bridge was over-engineered, for good reason. The original design by Thomas Bouch, engineer for the North British Railway Company, was rejected after his Tay Bridge collapsed in a storm with fatal consequences in 1879. The unfortunate Bouch, his reputation destroyed, died shortly after and was buried in the Edinburgh's Dean Cemetery.

Engineers Benjamin Baker and John Fowler and engineering contractor William Arrol were appointed. The work was hazardous. Memorials to 73 'briggers' who lost their lives during the six-year construction stand on South Queensferry's seawall promenade and on the north shore. The bridge was formally opened by the Prince of Wales.

Recent refurbishment included a specially formulated 'iconic Forth Bridge red' long-life paint, which laid off a team of painters employed to protect the steel structure from rust. Their labour coined the simile, 'like painting the Forth Bridge' meaning a never ending task. In 2015, the bridge was declared a UNESCO World Heritage Site.

# Index

1 Waterfront Avenue, Granton F 40
26BS (26 Bath Street), Portobello F 11
35 The Shore, Leith E 25
78–80 George Street B 43
112 Canongate A 7

Adam Smith's Panmure House A 6
Air Traffic Control Tower, Edinburgh Airport F 32
Archers Hall D 43
Arthur Lodge D 35
Assembly Rooms B 42
Augustine United Church A 57

Balmoral Hotel B 11
Bank of Scotland Headquarters A 40
Barclay Viewforth Church D 8
Bartholomew House D 34
Belford Hostel C 18
Black Castle, South Queensferry F 50
Bridgend Farm F 17
Burns Monument B 6

Cable Tramway Wheels E 14
Cables Wynd House E 10
The Café Royal B 12
The Caledonian Hotel C 4
Calton Jail Governor's House B 10
Cameron Toll Shopping Centre D 29
Cannonball House A 49
The Canny Man's D 19
Canongate Kirk A 9
Canongate Tolbooth A 10
Capital Building B 30
Caroline Park House F 39
Castle Terrace C 8
Central Library A 55
Central Mosque and Islamic Centre D 48
Chapel of St Albert the Great D 44
Charles Bell Pavilion, Astley Ainslie Hospital D 16
Charles II Monument A 35
Charlotte Chapel C 12
Charlotte Square B 49
Church Hill Theatre D 14
Church of Scotland Offices B 48
City Art Centre A 26
City Chambers A 31

City Observatory B 3
Colinton Parish Church F 27
Colinton Tunnel F 29
Corstorphine Doocot F 35
Corstorphine Old Parish Church F 36
Cowan's Warehouse B 13
Craigend Park F 18
Craigentinny Marbles F 3
Craiglockhart Hospital, Edinburgh Napier University F 23
Craigmillar Castle F 16
Craigsbank Church F 34
Cramond Harbour F 47
Cramond Kirk F 46

Dalmeny Kirk F 48
Dance Base A 53
Daniel Stewart's (Stewart's Melville) College C 21
David Hume statue A 38
Deacon Brodie's Tavern A 41
Dean Cemetery C 22
Dean Village C 23
The Democracy Cairn B 5
The Dome B 33
Dominion Cinema D 18
Donaldson's School C 17
Dovecot Studios A 69
Dr Bell's School E 11
Drummond House A 72
Drumsheugh Baths C 25
Duddingston Kirk F 1
Dugald Stewart Monument B 2
Dundas House B 23
Dynamic Earth A 4

Edinburgh Castle A 50
Edinburgh International Conference Centre C 10
Edinburgh Printmakers D 6
Edinburgh Sculpture Workshop E 4
Edinburgh Trades House C 16
The Ensign Ewart A 45
Eric Liddell Centre D 10
Exchange Buildings, Leith E 18

Fairmilehead Parish Church F 22
Falcon Hall Gates, Edinburgh Zoo F 38
Festival Theatre A 74
FetLor Youth Club C 41

# INDEX

Fettes College C 37
Fishmarket Square E 2
Fleshmarket Close A 29
The Forth Railway Bridge F 52
Fruitmarket Gallery A 25

George Heriot's School A 62
Gladstone Monument C 13
Gladstone's Land A 43
Gleneagles Townhouse B 25
Goose Pie House B 38
Grange House Wyverns D 32
Granton Castle Walled Garden F 44
Granton Gasworks Station F 41
The Grassmarket A 52
Greyfriars Bobby A 59
Greyfriars Charteris Centre D 49
Greyfriars Kirk A 58
Greyfriars Kirkyard A 60

Harrison Memorial Arch D 23
The Hawes Inn, South Queensferry F 51
Heave Awa' House A 19
Heriot-Watt College A 64
Hermitage of Braid D 21
Holyrood Abbey A 1
Holyrood Palace (The Palace of Holyroodhouse) A 2
Holy Trinity Church C 26
The Hub A 46

Institut Français Écosse A 39

Japanese House, Portobello F 10
Jenners B 28
John Knox House A 17
John Livingstone Memorial Stone D 11
Johnnie Walker Princes Street C 3
Jupiter Artland F 31

The Kilns, Portobello F 6
King's Theatre D 7
King's Wark E 24

Lady Stair's House (The Writers' Museum) A 42
Lamb's House, Leith E 20
Lammerburn D 13
Lauriston Castle F 45
Leith Central Station E 12

Leith Custom House E 23
Leith Fort E 5
Leith History Mural E 8
Leith Library and Theatre E 7
Leith Provident Co-operative Society E 9
Liberton Kirk F 19

The Mackenzie Mausoleum A 61
Madelvic House F 42
Maggie's Centre, Western General Hospital C 39
Malmaison Hotel, Leith E 27
Mansfield Traquair Centre B 20
The Manuscript of Monte Cassino sculptures B 17
Mayfield Salisbury Parish Church D 33
Meat Market Arches D 5
Melville Monument B 22
Mercat Cross A 34
The Merchants' Hall B 36
Merchiston Castle, Edinburgh Napier University D 12
Moray Place B 50
Morningside South Free Church D 20
Morocco Land A 14
Mortonhall Crematorium F 20
Moubray House A 17
The Museum of Edinburgh A 11

National Library of Scotland A 56;
National Library of Scotland D 38
National Monument of Scotland B 1
National Museum of Scotland A 63
National Records of Scotland, General Register House B 14
West Register House B 49
Nelson Monument B 4
The New Club B 37
Newhaven Harbour E 1
North Leith Parish Church E 6
Northern Lighthouse Board B 44
Nuffield Transplantation Surgery Unit C 40

Old Boroughmuir School D 9
Old Calton Burying Ground B 9
Old Fishmarket Close A 30
Old Parliament Hall A 36
Old St Paul's Episcopal Church A 22
Outlook Tower A 47
The Oxford Bar B 47

Patrick Geddes Centre A 44
Physicians' Hall B 35
Picardy Place B 18
Port of Leith Distillery E 31
Portobello and Joppa Parish Church F 8
Portobello Old Parish Church F 9
Portobello Police Station F 12
Portobello Swim Centre F 7
Prince of Wales Dry Dock Pumping Station, Leith E 30
Priory Church of St Mary of Mount Carmel, South Queensferry F 49
Prudential Assurance Building B 26

Quartermile D 1

Radisson Blu Hotel A 20
Raeburn House B 16
Raimes Clark & Co. E 13
Ramsay Garden A 48
Ramsay Lodge (Goose Pie House) B 38
Reid Memorial Church D 31
Richard Murphy House B 19
Riddle's Court (Patrick Geddes Centre) A 44
Robert Burns statue E 19
Robert Louis Stevenson House B 45
Robin Chapel F 14
Ronaldson's Wharf, Leith E 21
The Ross Fountain C 2
Rosslyn Chapel F 21
Royal Bank of Scotland Banking Hall B 24
Royal Botanic Garden:
   The Botanic Cottage C 33
   Front Range Glasshouses C 34
   Inverleith House C 32
   John Hope Gateway C 31
   Modern Alpine House C 36
   Temperate Palm House C 35
Royal Commonwealth Pool D 36
Royal High School B 7
Royal Hospital for Sick Children D 42
Royal Infirmary Buildings D 2
The Royal Observatory D 22
Royal Scots Greys Memorial B 40
Royal Scottish Academy B 39
The Royal Society of Edinburgh B 34
R W Forsyth Building B 27
Rutherford's Bar A 73
Rutland Square C 11

Saughton Park F 25
Schultz Chocolate Factory F 4
The Scotsman Building A 23
The Scotsman Steps A 24
The Scott Monument B 29
Scottish National Gallery B 39:
   Scottish National Gallery of Modern Art (Modern One and Modern Two) C 19
   Scottish National Portrait Gallery B 21
Scottish National War Memorial A 51
The Scottish Parliament A 3
Scottish Poetry Library A 8
Scottish Storytelling Centre A 16
Scottish Widows Building D 37
The Ship on The Shore, Leith E 26
Signet Library A 37
Social Bite Village F 43
South Bridge A 66
South Leith Parish Church Kirkyard E 15;
   South Leith Parish Church E 16
Southern Motors Filling Station D 39
Spylaw House F 28
St Andrew's Catholic Church C 20
St Andrew's Church B 32
St Andrew's House B 8
St Anne's Parish Church F 37
St Bennets Chapel D 15
St Bernard's Well C 27
St Cuthbert's Co-operative Society C 9
St Cuthbert's Episcopal Church F 26
St Cuthbert's Parish Church C 5
St Cuthbert's Poorhouse C 38
St Giles' High Kirk A 32
St James Quarter B 15
St John the Evangelist Catholic Church, Portobello F 13
St John's Church C 1
St Mary's Catholic Cathedral B 18
St Mary's Episcopal Cathedral C 14; St Mary's Song School C 15
St Ninian's Church and Manse, Leith E 22
St Patrick's Church A 68
St Paul's and St George's Episcopal Church B 18
St Peter's Church Morningside D 17
St Peter's Episcopal Church D 40
St Stephen's Stockbridge C 29
Standard Life Building B 31
Standard Life House C 6

Starbank House E 3
Stockbridge Colonies C 30
Stockbridge Library C 28
Suffolk Halls of Residence D 30
Sugarhouse Close A 12
Summerhall D 41
Surgeons' Hall and Museum A 75

The Tattoo Office A 28
The Thistle Chapel A 33
Thistle Foundation Centre of Wellbeing F 15
Thomson's Tower, Dr Neil's Garden F 2
Tollcross Community Fire Station D 4
The Tower, Portobello F 5
The Tron Kirk A 21
Trinity Apse A 18
Trinity House, Leith E 17
Tweeddale Court A 15

University of Edinburgh:
  Adam House A 65
  David Hume Tower D 45
  Edinburgh Climate Change Institute A 70
  The Fire Station (Edinburgh College of Art) D 3
  Gordon Aikman Lecture Theatre D 46
  Main Library D 45
  McEwan Hall D 51
  Moray House A 13

The Old College A 76
Old Infirmary Building A 71
Old Medical School D 52
Potterrow Project D 47
St Cecilia's Hall A 67
Teviot Row House D 50
  King's Buildings campus:
  Arcadia Nursery D 24
  Engineering Building D 28
  Noreen and Kenneth Murray Library D 26
  The Nucleus D 25
  Zoology Building D 27
The Usher Hall C 7

Victoria Quay E 32
Victoria Street A 54
Victoria Swing Bridge, Leith E 29

Walter Scott's Townhouse B 46
Water of Leith Visitor Centre F 24
Waverley Cafe A 27
The Wealth of Nations sculpture F 33
West Mill, Dean Village C 24
The Whalers' Memorial, Leith E 28
White Horse Close A 5
William Fraser Homes F 30
Wojtek the Soldier Bear B 41
The Writers' Museum A 42

## Acknowledgements

A big 'thank you' to my publisher Birlinn, especially to Hugh Andrew and Andrew Simmons for having faith in this book. Thanks also to the architects who answered questions, and to the people of Edinburgh. The best way to get to know the city is on the streets, for which this guide is intended. Special thanks to my wife Porta for her patience and encouragement, and for taking the photo of the Ross Fountain reproduced on page 94.

*Robin Ward* is an Edinburgh-based writer, architecture critic and graphic designer born and raised in Glasgow. An alumnus of Glasgow School of Art, he has worked for the *Herald* in Glasgow, the BBC in London and as architecture critic for *The Vancouver Sun*. He has written several books, among them the architectural guides *Exploring Vancouver* (he co-wrote three editions: 1993, 2012 and 2023) and *Exploring Glasgow* (2017).

# ON THE EDGE

## The Dwelling Hunter Series

Book 1

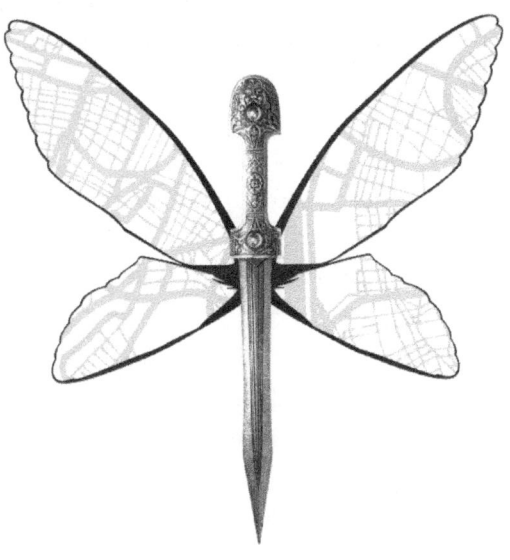

M. J. Glenn

Self-Published by Softwood Self-Publishing, Guildford, UK.

www.swspublishing.com

All rights reserved; no part of this publication may be reproduced or transmitted by any means, electronic, mechanical, photocopying, or otherwise, without the prior permission of the author.

First published in Great Britain in 2020

Copyright © Text M. J. Glenn 2020

ISBN 978-1-8381735-0-0

Any references to historical events, real people, or real places are used fictitiously. Names, characters, and places are products of the author's imagination.

Printed and bound in Great Britain by TJ Books
Cover design by Booksmith Designs